Building
Excellence
in Commercial
Negotiation

Counterpoint Courses
Building Excellence Series

Steve Mallaband
and
Ros Howard

Grosvenor House
Publishing Limited

This book is published by
Grosvenor House Publishing Ltd
28-30 High Street, Guildford, Surrey, GU1 3EL.
www.grosvenorhousepublishing.co.uk

A CIP record for this book
is available from the British Library

ISBN 978-1-78148-880-5

The companies Computalot and Drinkalot referred to
in this book are entirely fictional, and any resemblance
to real companies is entirely coincidental
and unintentional.

About Counterpoint Courses

Counterpoint Courses is a specialist consultancy and training business focused on procurement, communication and commercial negotiation. Its vision is to see a world where:

- People have the necessary communication skills to express their needs clearly and concisely, negotiate well and write effective contracts.

- Procurement is practised professionally such that the right goods and services are bought at the right price, right time and right quality.

- Suppliers are viewed as valuable assets of an organisation, and great care is taken to manage them well.

- Both procurement and sales professionals know how to negotiate good deals.

- Time and money are not wasted in fruitless negotiations, endless misunderstandings and problems with customers or suppliers.

More details can be found at www.counterpointcourses.com.

INTRODUCTION

The Counterpoint Courses *Building Excellence* series presents a concise summary of current best practice in the fields of procurement, communication and commercial negotiation. It is aimed both at those new to the subject and at those wishing to remind themselves of the fundamentals.

Each book within the series is designed to be easy to understand and easy to use. Unfortunately, the real world has a habit of getting in the way of simplicity, and adds a degree of complexity that prevents the use of the words "and easy to apply". Each book gives you the knowledge to go out into the real world, put into practice what you have learnt, make some mistakes, reflect on the good and the bad, and to keep trying until you really have mastered the subject. We call this *Building Excellence*, and it's well worth doing. The rewards for your organisation are high, as is the personal satisfaction of carrying out something to the best of your abilities.

This book – *Building Excellence in Commercial Negotiation* – is an exposition of the authors' conviction that by negotiating well you will be buying or selling things well, achieving the right price and the right relationship. It starts by setting out a negotiation scenario, involving the buying and selling of goods and services, and uses this throughout the book to illustrate the points made. The book starts by considering what negotiation is all about and why we negotiate. This is followed by sections on preparation for negotiation and then on the four-step negotiation process itself. Strategy and tactics are discussed, and the key role of the three different styles of behaviour is explored. The negotiation is not the end of the matter, of course, and the book concludes by discussing what has to happen next to ensure that there is a happy ending.

A set of appendices contains further information on certain topics, and also includes a list of books and other resources for those who want to explore the fascinating world of negotiation in more detail.

You cannot learn how to negotiate just by reading a book, and through the Counterpoint Courses organisation you can participate in one-, two- or three-day practical training sessions, which are based firmly around the experience gained by playing a negotiation game. Participants are divided into teams of buyers and sellers, and play a game where the aim is to negotiate the final agreement for the buying and selling of certain goods and services. Each team is coached, and the various rounds of the negotiation are interspersed with presentations, reflections, feedback and debate, to give participants a sound theoretical base to their learning.

CONTENTS

CHAPTER 1

Let's negotiate

INTRODUCTION

This book is equally useful to buyers and sellers but, to get us going, let us suppose you are a salesperson for Computalot, a medium-sized computer company, and you have recently submitted a bid for some computers (together with software, installation and maintenance) to Drinkalot Ltd. (who sell a range of fruit juices), to replace their existing accounting system. Drinkalot are also a medium-sized organisation, but they have recently been bought by an American company with headquarters in Dallas, Texas.

After a silence of some weeks, followed by a flurry of questions and answers, followed by yet another silence, you have just received a phone call to ask you to come to a meeting to discuss your bid. It appears that you have been shortlisted for consideration as a supplier in this case, and Drinkalot want to discuss things such as price, delivery and installation.

So, you stand on the verge of a negotiation.

But, just how did you get there? Did you put a good bid together? And, just what is negotiation and why do you need to negotiate? Why don't Drinkalot just accept your bid? Are there any other alternatives to negotiation here? And, if we have to negotiate, how can we negotiate well?

This book will answer these questions. It will show you how to negotiate good, sound commercial agreements, which deliver real value to your organisation.

So, let's get on with it, and learn how to negotiate well.

How do you get to a negotiation?

First, it is a good idea to ask just how Computalot and Drinkalot got to where they are now – on the brink of starting a negotiation.

Computalot followed their organisation's sales process, and, having identified Drinkalot as a potential customer, set about introducing themselves to Drinkalot about a year ago. They soon found out that Drinkalot were interested in a new accounting system, particularly one that could run the sort of advanced business analysis software that Computalot could provide. They took Drinkalot on a couple of reference visits to show them the quality of system they could offer and made it known that they would be very keen to bid, should an opportunity arise.

Drinkalot had followed their organisation's procurement process, and, having drawn up a specification for the new system, identified a longlist of ten potential suppliers. A quick review showed that only three were serious contenders: Computalot were one; an organisation who could provide a very similar system were another; and the third was in fact a software company that could provide the business analysis software but not the computer system behind it. However, the third contender had managed to find a computer systems company who were prepared to work together with them to deliver a complete system, and had submitted a joint bid. At this point, Drinkalot sent out an official invitation to tender, and got bids from all three potential suppliers.

Drinkalot analysed the bids and rapidly came to the conclusion that Computalot's was the most attractive. Yes, their price was higher; but the rest was just what they wanted, and Computalot had also provided some interesting options. Drinkalot's buyer felt that the price could be significantly reduced, knowing what they did about the market. Neither of the other bids was good: they were incomplete and unclear, and would take time to sort out.

So, Drinkalot invited Computalot to a first meeting, with the intention of pressing them very hard on price.

There is always a story about how you got to the negotiating table, and it is well worth understanding how the other party got there too. Buying and selling are subjects in their own right, but are covered briefly in appendix 2. If you want to know more about procurement, then Steve Mallaband and Ros Howard set out a good summary in *Building Excellence in Strategic Procurement Management* (Grosvenor House Publishing, planned early 2015). Likewise a good summary of the whole field of sales is contained in *SPIN-selling* (Gower Publishing Ltd., 1995) by Neil Rackham.

BUYERS AND SELLERS THINK DIFFERENTLY

It is also well worth understanding that buyers and sellers think differently, and knowing about this will help you negotiate better. These differences are covered in detail in appendix 2, and lead to some interesting opportunities that you should bear in mind when looking ahead to the negotiation:

- Sellers are often driven by the need to sell volume, and deals can be done that reward additional volume purchased with price reductions.

- Buyers are often driven by the need to make savings, and finding ways of helping the buyer to do this can be rewarding. Sellers should find out how the savings for a particular transaction will be measured, and present their bid in such a way that this maximises the savings made. Key to success here can often be the ability to ascribe a monetary amount to the otherwise hazy "additional value" contained in their bid. This is discussed further in chapter 3 and appendix 5 of this book.

- Sellers sometimes need to achieve half-year and year-end quotas, leading to opportunities to trade a price reduction for a quick sale.

- Buyers can get in early, before the sellers have even been approached, to make sure that a well-structured competitive bidding process takes place.

- Sellers can get in early, before the buyer is involved, and influence the business to buy their products on the basis that they are the only organisation that can satisfy the business's needs.

- Buyers can judge just how valuable the relationship is (usually less valuable than the seller claims), and ensure that the right price is attached to it.

- Sellers should learn the process the buyer has to go through to make the buying decision, and try to use its weak points to their advantage.

- Likewise, buyers should learn about the selling process and exploit its vulnerabilities.

WHAT MAKES A GOOD BID?

A good bid is necessary just to get to the negotiating table. And a discussion of your bid will in all likelihood form the opening of the negotiation event. Remember that your bid forms your opening position and, unless you are in a sealed bid or auction situation where negotiation is not allowed, you should expect to negotiate.

Research into negotiations and the observation of skilled negotiators in action suggest that a) the party which opens second is likely to have an advantage and b) if a party is forced to open first then they should open high, by stating their aims ambitiously. Thus your bid should be both attractive and ambitious. It should also be realistic, and you should be able to defend it if challenged.

When putting your bid together, you should:

- Try to find out who else is bidding, and use this knowledge to offer something that is better than or different from what the competition might bid. Consider also, where the competition might be able to offer something better than you can.

- Give your potential customer everything they asked for in the request for tender (or whatever they called the documents asking you to submit a bid).

- Make your bid easy for the buyer to read and understand. Professional buyers tend to look at the price first and then check that the bid includes everything asked for, before going on to the rest. Prices should appear alongside a list of deliverables, and not be hidden in the depths of the bid.

- Break down the price to a reasonable level of detail that matches a logical division of what is being sold. For example, Computalot could have included:

  ➤ Computer hardware.

  ➤ Printers.

  ➤ Business analysis software.

  ➤ Customisation of business analysis software.

  ➤ Initial consultancy.

  ➤ Project management.

  ➤ Installation.

  ➤ Testing and commissioning.

  ➤ Maintenance.

  ➤ Ongoing advice and consultancy.

- Make sure you include delivery dates and timescales.

- Include your key commercial terms. For example, Computalot could have included:

  ➢ Price: £850,000.

  ➢ Delivery: Schedule attached. Computers on site 8 weeks from order placement, installation and testing takes 4 weeks, subject to Drinkalot's readiness.

  ➢ Payment terms: 30 days from receipt of invoice.

  ➢ Stage payments: 30% on placement of order, 60% on delivery and 10% on completion of satisfactory installation and testing.

  ➢ Expenses: charged at cost.

  ➢ Intellectual property: any created during the provision of consultancy services belongs to Computalot.

  ➢ Standard terms of sale: these apply, copy attached.

- Clearly state any assumptions you have made in putting the bid together, particularly assumptions about things that are out of your control. For example, installation can only start if the buyer's site is ready.

- Present the solution asked for. Make it clear whether there are any parts of this you cannot provide, and provide alternative solutions, if you can, to fill these gaps.

- In addition, provide options and alternatives, particularly where the specification is at all vague. It may be that the buyer does not know exactly what they want, and that you can help by clarifying this.

- Lay out your bid clearly, using a structure that summarises what you are offering (including price) at the start, and then goes on to provide the details.

- Be complete, and avoid confusion and mistakes. Carefully remove all references to earlier bids when copying information across.

- Include supporting information, such as:

  ➢ The quality standards you work to.

  ➢ Names of existing customers.

  ➢ List of previous similar jobs (which could serve as a reference if required).

- Include only relevant information. There is nothing worse than a large amount of words that contains very little relevant information.

- Where what you are selling is difficult to define, and this can be the case with services, make sure it is clear just what is being offered. Try to explain the value provided by the service as well as its price, and try to quantify this value. For example, Computalot have included some days of project management in their bid, and this invites two challenges from Drinkalot. Firstly, "why does it need so many days, surely this is a simple job?" and, "why does project management cost so much per day?" Computalot should have tried to head off these challenges by providing supporting information in the bid.

- Where you are selling real talent or scarce skills, make this clear, price it accordingly and differentiate it from where you are selling things that most organisations in the market can sell. This is more relevant in areas such as management consultancy (where "thought-leaders" and "management gurus" command a premium price) and advertising (where "creative talent" is important). Make sure you explain (and quantify if at all possible) the extra value you get from paying more for top talent.

- Be clear just what you are selling, and price accordingly. In this case, are Computalot selling Drinkalot a computer system or are they selling them competitive advantage (through use of the business analysis software)?

There are also some other factors you should take into account when bidding:

- **Timing:** when to submit your bid depends on the type of bidding process. For example:

  ➢ Where competitive bidding proceeds by the use of sealed bids and no negotiation is allowed, then you can submit your bid any time before the closing deadline.

  ➢ However, if negotiation is allowed after the bidding, you should submit your bid as late as possible, to stop it being opened early and the "good bits" fed to the competitors.

  ➢ When competitive bids have been obtained, some buyers will try to play the bidders off against each other in a bid auction, in order to force down the price. If you suspect this is going to happen, and you cannot differentiate your bid from that of the competition in any meaningful way, then you should either bid as late as possible or not at all. Other possibilities might include having multiple options in your bid (to stop easy like-for-like comparisons), or approaching the buyer early, in private, with a lower offer only available if you win all the business.

- **Influencing:** you should consider whether there are any ethical ways you can influence the buyer to favour your bid. For example, by having big-name customers, arranging impressive reference visits, lobbying senior management within the buying organisation, stressing a long-term relationship, entertaining, socialising etc.

- **Consequences:** before submitting your bid consider what would happen if you didn't bid, if you bid and won, or if you bid and lost. Which is the best alternative?

WHAT IS NEGOTIATION?

"Negotiation is a tool. Just as a hammer is useful for driving nails, but not for driving golf balls, negotiation is useful for resolving some but not all disputes. It is useless if the parties have nothing in common to motivate settling their differences. It is unlikely to settle differences in belief, as the history of theological disputes testifies. It is even less likely to change Man's nature…" These are the opening lines from David Churchman's book *Negotiation: Process, Tactics, Theory* (University Press of America, 1995).

Thankfully, negotiation is a tool that is useful for solving problems concerning the terms and conditions under which goods, services or works are bought and sold. In this case the parties do have something in common: the seller wants to sell, and the buyer wants to buy.

Negotiation is a technique that relies on trading to define the outcome. It proceeds via a series of trades such as, "if you buy maintenance from us for the next three years, we would be prepared to lower our price for the computers," or, "if you want us to include consultancy, then we would charge that at our standard rate." You trade because you hold things that the other party does not, and because the other party needs what you have. Here, Computalot holds the computers, and Drinkalot needs a new accounting system.

You also trade because you value things differently. Here, Computalot might value selling maintenance more highly than selling the computers at a high price, because they make more profit on maintenance than they do on computers. Computalot could offer a lower price for the computers in return for Drinkalot committing to three years' maintenance. This would suit Drinkalot, because they haven't much cash and would prefer to pay as little as possible right now; they value the lower price for the computers now more than having to pay for three years' maintenance, the money for which can be found from next year's budget.

Negotiation is not a technique that provides a right answer. There is often no right answer to the matter under consideration, but a range of possible outcomes. In this case, Computalot has quoted a fixed price for the computers, but in fact they could go lower and still make their target profit on the deal. They could also be persuaded to lower their price, for example, if they could be certain that Drinkalot would buy the maintenance for the computers from Computalot for the next three years.

WHAT DO YOU NEED TO NEGOTIATE?

In simple cases, a negotiated agreement will need to be reached on basic commercial terms such as:

- **Specification:** what exactly are the goods/services/works to be supplied?

- **Quality/Standards of Performance:** to what quality standards should goods be supplied or services/works be performed?

- **Volumes:** how much will be delivered during the length of the contract? Is there a commitment to buy a certain volume?

- **Price:** how much will the buyer pay to acquire the goods/services/works?

- **Payment Terms:** when is the price to be paid?

- **Delivery and Timings:** where, when and how are the goods/services/works to be delivered? When does the contract start and how long will it last?

However, in more complex cases, agreement will need to be reached on many other issues too. A more comprehensive list is given at the end of appendix 5.

WHY DO YOU NEGOTIATE?

We negotiate because it is a good way of solving certain problems. In solving these problems, it makes us better off. Drinkalot will be better off with the new accounting system than they would be if they kept the old one, which breaks down regularly and in any case cannot perform the sophisticated financial analysis demanded in today's business environment. Computalot will be better off because they earn money from the sale.

ALTERNATIVES TO NEGOTIATION

Negotiation is not the best way of solving all problems, by any means, and there are many alternatives. In the commercial world of buying and selling, however, negotiation is often a good choice for deciding the deal.

In this case, Drinkalot did have some alternatives. It could have said, "yes," to Computalot's bid, and just bought on the terms and conditions on offer. This is unlikely to be the best strategy if there are a number of organisations that could supply the accounting system, as fostering competition between them can help to drive a better deal. On the other hand, if Computalot is the only supplier in the market, and offers business on a take-it-or-leave-it basis, then saying, "yes," would have made sense.

Saying, "no," was another possibility and presumably Drinkalot would have done this and gone elsewhere, had Computalot's bid not been attractive in some way.

Computalot and Drinkalot could also have sat down together and indulged in some joint problem solving, with the idea of, "if you bare your soul to me, then I'll bare my soul to you," so to speak. This is all very well if there is a high degree of trust between the parties and no danger that one party would take advantage of the other. Even if there were, there would need to be the willingness to share what might be commercial secrets (costs and budgets for example), and even this would not resolve issues where Computalot and Drinkalot held fundamentally different points of view about the value of certain items under discussion.

THE NEGOTIATION GAME

Negotiation is best regarded as a game where you start with two solutions, your own and that of the other party. The aim is to find a third solution, which satisfies both parties, and in that sense there is no single best outcome (no right answer) and no winners or losers: winning and losing lies mostly in the minds of the players. The game can be complex, and people approach it in all sorts of different ways. Negotiation has few rules: physical force is not allowed, and bribery and corruption are severely frowned upon. Apart from that, virtually anything goes.

The game does follow a definite process, however:

- **Opening bid:** the seller makes an opening bid, as part of some kind of tendering process, as discussed above.

- **Preparation:** both parties do their homework. They make sure they know what they are trying to achieve, what they have to negotiate with and where the power lies. They also try to find out as much as possible as they can about the other party and its strengths and weaknesses.

- **The negotiation event:** the parties meet and the negotiation event, as it is called, begins. This follows a definite four-step process, which leads slowly but surely (and via much iteration) from disagreement to agreement.

- **Behaviour during the negotiation:** during the process, there are three key behaviours that must be mastered to ensure success. There are also some useful tactics that need to be learnt, and you need to know how to defend yourself against some of the tricks and traps (known as ploys) that the other party might use against you.

- **Agreement and beyond:** at the end of the process, agreement is reached and documented.

A review of the negotiation is carried out by each party, in order to assess how well they think they performed and to capture lessons for the future. The agreement reached must then be implemented, and the inevitable change that the future brings must be dealt with.

KEY INGREDIENTS FOR SUCCESS IN NEGOTIATION

The following factors usually have the most influence on the outcome of the negotiation game:

- **Quality of opening bid:** a good bid from the seller maximises the chances of being considered for business in the first place; it is necessary just to get to the negotiating table. It also sets the tone for any negotiation that follows.

- **Preparation:** those who prepare well usually do better. Thorough preparation is that part of negotiation where one party may ethically gain an advantage over the other.

- **Power:** the party that has more power to influence the course of events usually does better than the other party, unless it abuses that power.

- **Expectations:** those who aim high usually do better than those who don't.

- **Skill of the negotiator:** skilled negotiators do better than unskilled ones. Negotiation is a skill that can be learnt.

WHAT MAKES A GOOD NEGOTIATOR?

Good negotiators do the following things well:

- **Attitude:** they have a positive, optimistic attitude and have high expectations for the outcome.

- **Negotiating behaviour:** they use the three negotiating behaviours appropriately, and at the right time.

- **Communication:** they communicate well, asking the right questions and listening carefully to the answers.

- **Use of power:** they understand where the power lies and how to use it; they do not abuse its use.

- **Process:** they clearly understand the four-step negotiation process and how it flows.

- **Use of tactics:** they understand the range of tactics available and which ones work best under what circumstance; they can deploy these effectively.

- **Countering of ploys:** they understand what traps can be sprung, what tricks can be played on the unwary and what games can be played to gain an advantage. They have the ability to counter these effectively.

- **Relationship:** They have the ability to get the balance right between the result achieved and the relationship between the parties that it creates.

PLAYING THE NEGOTIATION GAME WELL

There is definitely a best way to play the negotiation game: a way to get the best deal for your organisation that you can. By concentrating your attention on the key ingredients for success listed above and by mastering the skills that make a good negotiator, you will maximise your chances of doing well.

The rest of the book will show you how to do this by taking you through the whole of the negotiation process, and illustrating this by showing how Computalot and Drinkalot manage to craft a final deal.

First, however, there is some theory to be covered, and this is set out in chapter 2. Some people like to know something about how a game works before they start playing it, and this chapter is for them. Others prefer to jump straight in and get on with it, preferring to learn the theory as and when they need it; if you are one of these, then you should move straight to chapter 3 and come back (and dip into) chapter 2 at leisure. Some people of course, jump straight in and seem to absorb the theory as they go along, with little help from books; if you are one of these, then please feel free to ignore chapter 2 completely.

In chapter 3, negotiation proper is returned to, and the importance of preparation is discussed.

Then, in chapter 4, behaviour, tactics and ploys are explored, and you will learn just how you can play the negotiation game well. You need to know this before you meet the other party and the negotiation event starts in earnest

In chapter 5, the negotiation event is dissected, and the steps of the negotiation process itself are explained. This comes to an end when agreement is reached, or sometimes when the parties walk away, having failed to find enough common ground.

Although the negotiation proper is now at an end, this is only the beginning in one sense. You have just negotiated an agreement, but now you must be committed to implement it; the courtship and wedding are over, now you must live with your partner.

Although this is not the main focus of this book, it is covered briefly in chapter 6.

In conclusion, a summary of what you should have learnt is presented in chapter 7 – Negotiation in a nutshell.

Epilogue

In this first chapter, the questions posed by Computalot's salesperson right at the start have been answered, and you have been brought back to the point where Computalot must prepare for the negotiation to come. In summary:

- The buying and selling processes are different, as are the mindsets of buyers and sellers.

- Make sure you put in a good bid: attractive, ambitious, realistic and defendable.

- Negotiation is a tool that helps you solve a problem or resolve an issue.

- Negotiation is a tool that is ideally suited for deciding the terms and conditions on which goods/services/works are bought and sold. There are many alternatives to negotiation as a means of solving problems, and these have their place elsewhere.

- Negotiation works by trading something you have for something you want.

- Negotiation is best seen as a game with relatively few rules and no real winners or losers. It is a game however that follows a definite process.

- There is definitely a best way to play the negotiation game and this can readily be learnt.

CHAPTER 2

Some essential theory

INTRODUCTION

You have an idea that you might be able to negotiate better, if you understood some of the theory behind negotiation. You know that theory is sometimes boring but you realise that, like most things in life, there is no gain without pain and, as you learn, it just might be that everything becomes illuminated.

For example, you've heard of win-win (and lose-lose), but what do these terms really mean? How can you measure the success of a negotiation, and doesn't the outcome depend on the relationship in any case?

Let's cover these points in a bit more detail.

WIN-LOSE, WIN-WIN AND OTHER TYPES OF NEGOTIATION

A simple way of looking at the outcome of a negotiation is shown in the following diagram:

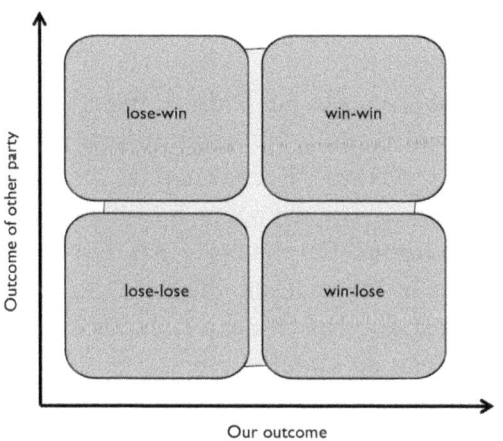

Diagram 1 – Negotiation outcomes

Referring to the diagram, you can see that it is possible to pigeonhole the possible outcomes of a negotiation into four categories as follows:

- **Win-lose:** this is where one party (say the buyer) gets what they want (a low price, for example) but the other (the seller) does not. This is the result of what is known as a distributive or fixed-pie negotiation. In this type of negotiation the size of what is being negotiated is fixed. For example, if Computalot were simply offering to sell a single, well-defined computer for a fixed price then all there is to talk about is the price of the computer. What Computalot gain by selling at a higher price, Drinkalot loses by having to pay the higher price. It is like having to share a pie with your friend. The size of the pie is fixed and you are both hungry. If you take a bigger share, then your friend gets a smaller share. What one party gains, the other party loses, and this type of negotiation is often called a zero-sum game.

  Sometimes you hear the term, "mythical fixed pie", which is a way of encouraging you to look as hard and as wide as possible for other possibilities to trade, in order to avoid a win-lose outcome. It's like coming up with some chips to go with the pie, and being able to offer your friend more chips to make up for the lack of pie.

  Sometimes, however, the pie really is fixed in size. In cases of extreme material scarcity, or when an organisation has been able to close a market (by commercial monopoly or patent protection) there is often little a buyer can do to influence terms and conditions. On the other hand, where there is a lot of competition in the market, the buyer is able to play one seller off against another to achieve better terms and there is little the seller can do about it.

- **Win-win:** this is where both parties feel they have achieved their aims, and are satisfied with the result. This is the result of what is known as an integrative negotiation. In this case, the idea is to find ways to expand the pie so that there is enough for everyone to have a satisfying share. It involves broadening the field under consideration, looking for options, and perhaps collaborating to find a solution. For example, Computalot are offering to sell several computers and also installation services and maintenance. By including for instance a couple of computers that are not needed for another six months, they might be able to sell the computers at a lower price and sell some installation services too. They win because they have sold more computers and some services as well, and Drinkalot wins because they get at a lower price some computers they would need anyway in six months' time, and installation would have cost them a fortune had they done it themselves. Both parties gain; this type of negotiation is known as a positive-sum game.

- **Lose-win:** This is the opposite of win-lose. This time the seller gets what they want (a high price, for example) but the buyer does not.

- **Lose-lose:** This is where the negotiation deadlocks or breaks down without a result, and neither party wins. Or, sometimes, where agreement is actually reached but neither party is happy with it.

In practice, however, things are not that simple: the pie is often partly fixed, and the negotiation becomes a mixture of value creating and value claiming. The expanded pie may still not be big enough to share to the real satisfaction of both parties, and the relationship between the parties comes into it too. There are a myriad of intermediate cases, depending on to what extent the buyer or seller gets what they want, and these range from win-partial win all the way down to lose-partial lose.

There is another case, too, where a buyer, for example, is convinced that they have achieved a good price, but in fact they have just been persuaded that this is the case by an expert seller. In this case the outcome is "win-thought they'd won". Or in the opposite case, where a buyer convinces a seller that they've done well to make the sale, when in fact the seller has sold at a price massively lower than the nearest competition.

Although this model is useful, it should be remembered that the outcome of a negotiation is at least partly subjective and what one party regards as a success, another might regard as a failure. For example, in price negotiations with a large buyer, one seller may regard the achievement of a price that allows them to make a minimal profit as a major success since their experience of dealing with similar large buyers in the past has always been worse. Another seller may feel that achieving this same price is a failure, as in fact it represented a decrease in price compared to last year. Here we have the same outcome being judged as win-win and win-lose.

In what is known as vertical relationships between buyers and sellers, where goods/services/works are simply bought and sold, and there is little operational cooperation between the parties, the negotiation is more likely to be of a value claiming nature. Where a number of suppliers have been prequalified and meet the basic requirements for trade in terms of specification, quality, volume and delivery time, then the discussion will concentrate on price and the words win and lose are almost irrelevant. For example, at the first meeting with Drinkalot, Computalot might start by emphasising the wonders of their solution and how it will transform the future of Drinkalot. However, they could find themselves faced with a professional buyer from Drinkalot who says, "you wouldn't be here at all if you couldn't sell us what we want, your quality wasn't good and you couldn't deliver on time. What we're here for is to talk about price."

Under such circumstances, it is worth questioning whether a true win-win can actually be achieved in practice.

CAN A TRUE WIN-WIN EVER BE ACHIEVED?

On the face of it, the win-win outcome is the most attractive, but there can be significant problems in achieving it. One way to proceed would be to treat the problem of how to determine the commercial terms for a transaction in which goods/services/works are bought and sold as one requiring a joint collaborative solution. The premises here are, "if we work together then we will both do better," and, "by judiciously sharing information and brainstorming, we will seek to expand the pie so that each side may get as much as possible of what they would like."

There are some severe obstacles to this approach, as discussed earlier, when we talked about the alternatives to negotiation in chapter 1 of this book. However, such an approach does work well in what are known as horizontal commercial relationships, where a commercial deal has already been reached and where the parties then work together operationally to develop a new product, to reduce product costs or to increase supply-chain efficiency. These activities can indeed be win-win and deliver value to both parties, but it is wise to agree the basis on which the value created will be shared before the joint activity begins.

If you want to know more about the theory behind win-win, and its strengths and weaknesses, Andrew Cox presents a good summary in *Win-Win?* (Earlsgate Press, 2004). In addition, David L Sheridan sets out a realistic critique of the win-win approach in the opening chapter of his book *Negotiating Commercial Contracts* (McGraw-Hill, 1991).

In order to navigate your way through the win-win minefield, it helps to have a way of measuring outcome, so that you have some objective idea of how you have done, and not just a feeling that you've either won or lost.

MEASURING OUTCOME

Measuring outcome objectively is not easy. You can try to do this, for example, by comparing the outcome to what happened earlier, when you sold similar things to similar customers in a similar market. Or you could measure how well you are doing compared to the competition: do you win more deals than they do? And if they win a deal, do you know why and on what terms they did so?

The other point to think about is the relationship between the parties and to what extent this comes into the equation when you are looking for the best outcome.

OUTCOME VERSUS RELATIONSHIP

If Drinkalot persist with their determination to focus on price, Computalot can always goes down the route of suggesting, "if you push too hard on the price, you will spoil the relationship." And with spoiling the relationship comes the threat that service will not be good and you won't get any favours from us... This is likely to impress Drinkalot's finance manager, the person who has to live with the consequences of the purchase, more than it is likely to impress a professional buyer. Yes, there is a trade-off to be made between deal and relationship, but if Computalot are interested in repeat business then they are hardly likely to offer poor service.

In the extreme of a one-off purchase, where the parties are unlikely to do business together again, then relationship is of little consequence and the deal is everything. This is perhaps why second-hand car dealers have such bad name. At the other extreme, when close collaboration is required to ensure a successful outcome, the relationship is extremely important. For example, if you were selling advertising, then Drinkalot would want to make sure that they could work together with you creatively at an operational level, to ensure that their fruit juice was marketed as well as possible. Personal "chemistry" would come into play, and the quality of the relationship would have a higher value.

In fact, you should ask yourself the question right at the start as to just what relationship you want with the other party. This depends to some extent on the market, as can be seen from the following diagram:

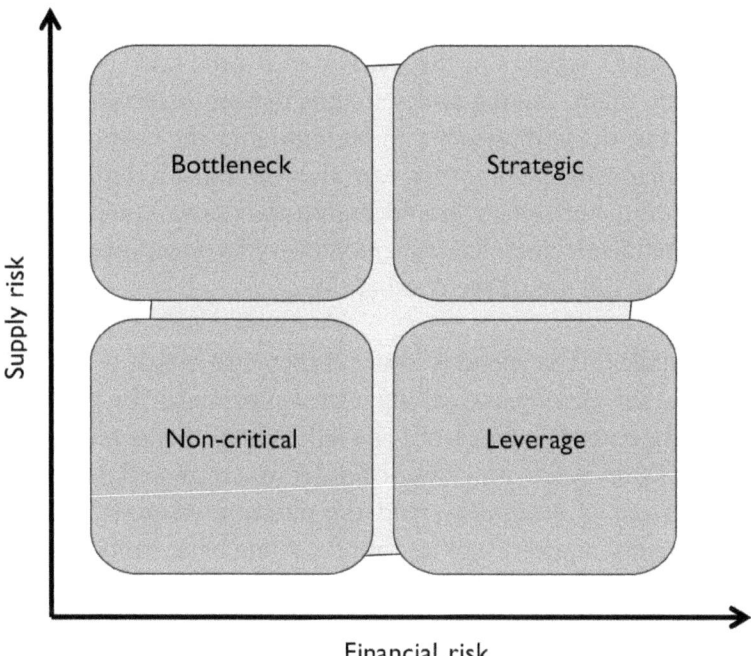

Diagram 2 – The Sourcing Category Positioning (Kraljc) Matrix

The diagram looks at the market from a buyer's point of view, and categorises what is to be bought into four possibilities, depending on the financial risk (usually measured by spend) and the supply risk (usually measured by the scarcity of suppliers in the market or the dependency of the organisation on the suppliers). Referring to the diagram, you can see that it is possible to pigeonhole suppliers into four categories as follows:

- **Strategic:** Here the spend is high and there are few suppliers in the market. It may be a good strategy for a buyer and seller to form a longer term strategic relationship in order to maximise mutual value from the relationship. However, the basis for this must always be rooted in a good commercial agreement. Strategic relationships can be called "partnerships" but the term is often misused and whole area is difficult. It is dealt with further in appendix 3.

- **Leverage:** The spend is still high, but there are now a reasonable number of suppliers in the market and some real competition between them. Buying and selling is driven to some extent by price, but the complexity can be high, and the cost of change from one seller to another can also be high. Relationship is important, but sellers should realise that buyers will want to go to tender, if not each year then every two to three years, to maximise the use of the competition.

- **Non-critical:** The spend is low and there are lots of suppliers in the market. Buying and selling is driven primarily by price, and since the cost of change from one seller to another is usually low, relationship is not very important. A much-quoted example is the buying of stationery, and the extreme example is a true commodity market, such as that for some basic foodstuffs and raw materials. Here there will be a separate "exchange", such as the London Metal Exchange, where the goods are bought and sold at the market price.

- **Bottleneck:** The spend is low but there are few suppliers in the market, and sometimes only one. The price is set primarily by the supplier and there is little room for negotiation. The supplier will usually offer a good relationship to mask the harsh commercial reality of the situation. A good example here is Microsoft; there are few alternatives to Windows.

There are of course a myriad of intermediate cases, depending on exactly what is going on in the market, but the use of this matrix can avoid relationship blunders. Sellers tend to overvalue relationship, and the above clearly shows that where the value is low and there is a lot of competition, relationship is worth little to a buyer. On the other hand, buyers tend to underestimate relationship, and where there is a genuine need to cooperate on an operational level to generate value from a relationship, then buyers should remember that relationship is important.

Most commercial deals are struck in markets that fall somewhere between the extremes of commodity and genuinely strategic. In such cases, relationship does matter, but it is only when one party feels significantly exploited by the other that it causes real problems. Inappropriate, seemingly unfair, unethical or illegal agreements have a habit of coming back to bite the party who perhaps used too much power, or too much trickery, to agree them.

The best commercial relationships are those that both parties enter into at their own free will and with their eyes fully open as to the advantages and disadvantages that they bring. Both parties also need to realise that things will change; that the change will need managing; and, that this can then change the nature of the relationship. They also need to remember that, sooner or later, the relationship will end. If you can enter business relationships in this spirit, as either buyer or seller, then you have gone a long way to solving the relationship problem.

Finally, a word of caution: relationships based on trust and good intentions can be very fragile and are easily invaded and exploited by parties who do not possess these qualities. A sound commercial contract should always be in place to document the commercial relationship, if nothing else. Even a good contract, however, will not protect you against a party with power who tears up the contract later on the grounds that circumstances have changed, and insists on "renegotiating" the terms.

Epilogue

In this chapter you have learnt some of the theory behind negotiation, so that you can better understand what lies ahead. In summary:

- In the extreme, negotiations can be win-win (value creating) or win-lose (value claiming).

- In practice, however, they range all the way from win-win through win-partly win and partly win-lose to lose-lose.

- There are no real winners or losers in a negotiation and another important outcome is win-thought they'd won.

- True win-wins are much more likely to be achieved in strategic relationships, once the commercial deal has been fully hammered out.

- In some commercial deals everything boils down to price, and the outcome can be win-lose.

- Look for all possible ways to expand the pie; it gives a better chance of finding a win-win.

- Measure the outcome of a negotiation objectively if you can, and try to understand whether you did better than last time.

- Relationship can be important as well as outcome, but remember that relationship has little value in a highly competitive market.

CHAPTER 3

Preparation – gathering the facts

INTRODUCTION

You understand now how you got to where you are – the bidding process, and have some idea about what lies ahead – the negotiation. You've read the boring bit about theory and digested at least some of it.

Reflecting on your bid, you feel that this was good enough. You took time to research the requirements; you made some suggestions, and priced a few options that you feel should be attractive. Your pricing was ambitious, but not unreasonably so, and you do have a quality product. There are very few companies that have the expertise to implement the financial analysis software you have proposed.

The bid certainly must have been attractive in some way, as you've been invited to a meeting with Drinkalot, and this meeting almost certainly signals the start of the negotiation event.

The next on the list is the need for good and thorough preparation. But what exactly does this mean? What should you be preparing, and just how should you go about it?

Let's consider these points in a bit more detail.

THE NEED FOR GOOD PREPARATION

Good preparation is essential to success in negotiation. It is carried out as a discrete stage, prior to the negotiation event itself, and nothing in the later stages can compensate for poor preparation, nor can a highly skilled negotiator make up for a lack of it.

If you do not prepare, you will be reduced to working from suppositions and guesswork, instead of from hard facts and reasoned assumptions. You should not forget that the other party will do its preparation too and, if you do not prepare, you will concede considerable power to them even before the negotiation event itself begins.

Preparation is a chance to consider what you have to trade, what your alternatives are and where the power lies. It is also a chance to try to look at things from the other party's point of view, and to find out as much as you can about them and how they will view the negotiation. It involves fact-finding and information gathering and, where hard facts are difficult to come by in a reasonable time, it includes making educated guesses and reasonable assumptions.

It is also an opportunity to check your aims and objectives, formulate your strategy and make your plans.

WHAT SHOULD YOU PREPARE?

Preparation should address the questions posed by Rudyard Kipling in his story *The Elephant's Child:*

> "I keep six honest serving-men:
> (They taught me all I knew)
> Their names are What and Why and When
> And How and Where and Who."

- **Why are you negotiating?** What are your aims and objectives? What do you want? What do you need?

- **Who are you negotiating with?** Who is in their team? What are their backgrounds, personalities and culture? Do they have the authority to negotiate? Indeed, who is in your team, what are their roles and do you have the authority to negotiate?

- **What do you know about the market and the competition?** What's the market like? Who is the likely competition?

- **Where does the power lie?** Do you have the power, or does the other party?

- **What are you negotiating?** What have you bid? What do you have to trade? What alternatives do you have?

- **When will the negotiation event take place?** When is the first meeting? Is more than one meeting likely to be necessary? How long might it all take? Do you have any deadlines?

- **Where will the negotiation event take place?** Where will the event take place? What arrangements are needed for rooms and refreshments? Will you be away from home? Is there a chance for informal discussions?

- **How do you want to conduct the negotiation?** What is your strategy? What are your plans? How will you communicate? Which tactics will you use?

WHY ARE YOU NEGOTIATING? – AIMS AND OBJECTIVES

In our example, Computalot are about to negotiate with Drinkalot, and the aim of the negotiation is to determine the terms and conditions that govern the sale of a computer system. As we have seen, there is no right answer to a negotiation, and thus there is no one set of terms and conditions that satisfy the aim of the negotiation.

From Computalot's point of view, you could say that their aim is to achieve the best result for Computalot, and from Drinkalot's point of view, you could say that their aim is to achieve the best result for Drinkalot. But nobody is trying to win – remember that the negotiation game has no winners or losers – so why shouldn't Computalot have as its aim to try to achieve the best possible result for itself, while at the same time achieving the best possible result for Drinklalot?

This is in fact a better outcome for Computalot, as not only do they feel good about the result, but so do Drinkalot. Such an outcome is called a "win-win," as we learnt in chapter 2. It's not always possible, as we also learnt, particularly if the negotiation just boils down to a discussion about one item – price. It remains, however, a laudable overall aim.

A problem of course with the above aim is that it is not very clear; the word "best", for example, is not defined. It's fine to have such broad statements of what you want to achieve, but they need to be backed up with some objectives. These are more detailed measurable milestones that allow you to assess in a more accurate way whether you have achieved your aims.

You should remember a couple of points about objectives here:

- **SMART:** your objectives should be SMART – Specific, Measurable, Achievable, Realistic and Time-constrained.

- **Wants and needs:** when thinking about your objectives, you should be careful to distinguish between wants and needs. You should try to negotiate from need and not from greed.

This is also the time to think about your strengths and weaknesses, and those of the other party; it is a good idea to carry out a SWOT analysis (Strengths, Weaknesses, Opportunities and Threats) with particular reference to the negotiation to come.

For example, Computalot could have come up with the following aim, objectives and SWOT analysis:

- **Aim:** To negotiate the sale of the financial computer system ("Project Accountalot") to Drinkalot Ltd. on the best possible terms.

- **Objectives:**

  ➢ To complete the deal by 30 June (in two months' time), in order to be able to book the sale in the first half-year results.

> ➢ To achieve at least 20% of contract price up front and payment terms of 30 days.

> ➢ To achieve an overall price of £750,000 (excluding separately priced option), which represents a gross margin (sale price minus costs) of 21%.

> ➢ To sell at least three years of support and maintenance as part of the initial deal (five years is included as an option in the bid).

> ➢ To create a relationship where it is judged that Drinkalot is likely (80% certainty) to come back to Computalot for all future modifications to the system and to buy maintenance for the estimated life of the system (ten years).

> ➢ To sell at least 28 days of consultancy as part of the original deal (60 days was included as an option in the bid).

- **SWOT analysis:**

Strengths:

> ➢ **Can offer complete system:** including hardware, software, installation, maintenance, consultancy and business support.

> ➢ **Leader in the field:** one of only three organisations in the country who can provide the business analysis software. Of the other two, only one can provide a complete system.

> ➢ **Alternative:** there is a good prospect of selling a similar system to another organisation on similar timescales. This means there is an alternative, and alternatives mean power.

Weaknesses:

> ➢ **Expensive:** Computalot position themselves at the high end of the market and so the system is likely to be more highly priced than that of any competitor.

➢ **Short of cash:** although Computalot is profitable, most of their cash has been ploughed into software development. They need to achieve favourable stage payments and avoid long payment terms.

➢ **First half year:** Computalot needs to sell a system within the next two months (even if not to Drinkalot) in order to show investors steady sales progress.

Opportunities:

➢ **First customer:** Drinkalot would be the first customer in the drinks industry; they would be a good reference and open up sales potential in this market.

➢ **Full power of software:** Drinkalot want to use the full power of the business analysis software, something that other customers to date have not done. The opportunity for Computalot to prove they can successfully implement a more complex system is valuable.

➢ **New computers:** Computalot's IT people are keen to try out some new high-speed computers, which they believe will enhance the capability of the system.

Threats:

➢ **Catch up on lead:** other organisations wanting to catch up on Computalot's lead in business analysis software may offer very attractive pricing just to get the experience.

➢ **Untested computers:** the new computers have not yet been tried in the field, although they perform well under test conditions.

➢ **Buying separately:** if Drinkalot picks the system to pieces by buying the hardware, software, installation and consultancy separately, they could potentially make significant savings.

WHO ARE YOU NEGOTIATING WITH?

You need to decide who is in your team and learn who will be in the other party's. You shouldn't guess, but should simply ask the other party who will be there and what their role will be. There are no real rules on who should be in a negotiating team or not, but common sense dictates that there should be as few as possible, consistent with having the necessary knowledge to carry out the negotiation.

There are some points, however, that you should always consider:

- **Who:** who will be there at the negotiation event? What are the names, positions and roles of both your team and their team? Do you know the other party and the members of their team? Have you dealt with them before? What do you know about them from this experience: their personalities and their cultural backgrounds?

- **Who else:** who else needs to be involved in your organisation, and what is the level of their involvement? This will almost certainly include your boss, who will at least need to be informed of what is going on. But are there any other stakeholders, and what are their roles?

- **Roles:** who is the lead negotiator and what are the roles of the other members of the team? In commercial negotiations, the responsible buyer and responsible salesperson, respectively, usually take this role, but in high-value or particularly sensitive areas this role could be fulfilled by external specialists. You should remember that the skill of the lead negotiator is a major factor in negotiation success, and that this role is normally best left to well-trained and experienced staff.

- **Alignment:** is your negotiation team aligned? Does each member know and understand their role, and are the aims and objectives of the negotiation clear? This is the time to check; not during the negotiation event itself.

- **Authority:** do you as a team have the authority to negotiate, or will reference always have to be made to other stakeholders when key decisions have to be made. Are there limits to your authority? Would Computalot's team have to check back with the finance director, for example, to determine whether it would be possible to accept a sales margin of less than the objective of 21%? What about the limits to the authority of Drinkalot's team?

- **Approvals process:** who has to approve the deal, for both the buyers and the sellers? What is the approval process, and does it take time?

For example, Computalot's team could consist of:

- **A. Senior Salesperson:** as lead negotiator.

- **A.N. Applications Expert:** who knows all about the business analysis software Computalot is offering.

- **A.N. IT Person:** who can answer any technical questions about the computer system.

Computalot should make sure their team is authorised to complete the negotiation. For example, this could well be the case for outcomes in line with the objectives set out above. However, they may well have to refer back to both the sales director and finance director for permission to move beyond these.

And they should find out who Drinkalot will be bringing to the table. This could well be:

- **A. Buyer:** as lead negotiator, the member of the purchasing function who sent out the request for tender.

- **A. User:** the member of the finance function who will ultimately be responsible for the system.

- **A.N. IT Person:** who will want to ask all sorts of technical questions about the system.

Computalot will have met A. User of course, as they took them on the reference visits. A.N. IT Person tagged along on one of these visits too, but although they have dealt with A. Buyer during the bid process, they have never met in person. A. Buyer always seemed very busy and although a lot of questions were asked about the bid, these were not very searching in nature. Computalot may well not be at all sure of Drinkalot's authority to negotiate, particularly as the involvement of their new American parent is unclear.

WHAT DO YOU KNOW ABOUT THE MARKET AND THE COMPETITION?

All buying and selling takes place in a market, and to a greater or lesser extent it is the market that determines price and not the cost of the goods. You need to understand something of the dynamics of the market in which you are buying and selling before you can go out and negotiate a good deal. Understanding the market means understanding the competition too. What works in a buyer's market (where there is surplus capacity and/or a lot of competition), for example, won't work in a seller's market (where demand is chasing restricted supply and/or there are very few suppliers capable of meeting the demand).

There are two diagrams that are helpful here. The first – the Sourcing Category Positioning Matrix – we have seen before, under the discussion on relationships. This helps you think about suppliers in the market as being one of four possible types: strategic, leverage, non-critical or bottleneck. The second is known as Porter's Five Forces and is drawn below:

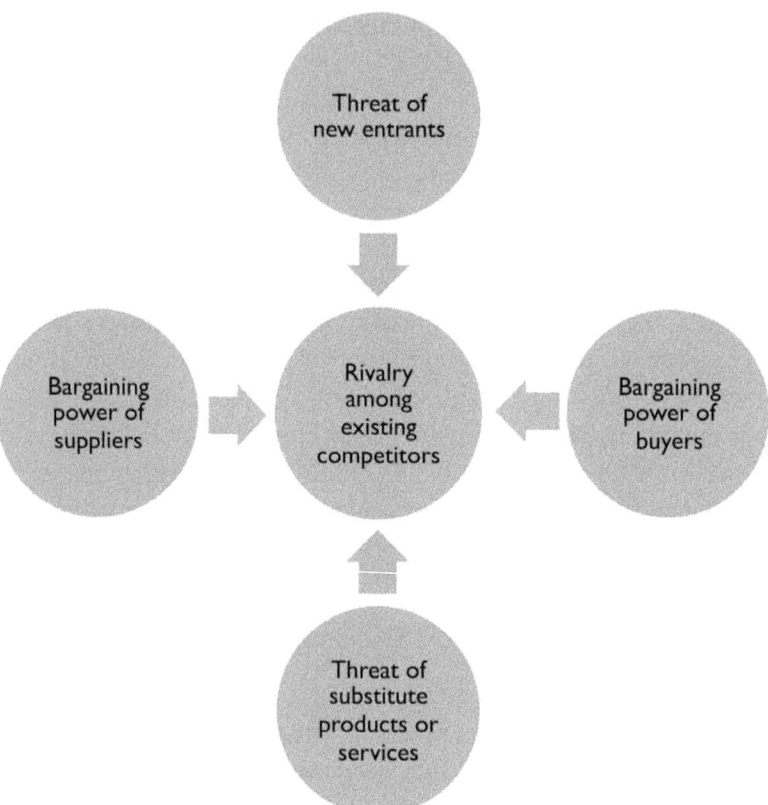

Diagram 3 – Porter's Five Forces

This shows that in any market there are five separate forces at work. Knowing about these helps you to think more clearly about the nature of the market and of the competition. These forces are:

- **Competitive rivalry:** this concerns how the competitors in a market deal with each other and how the competition between the competitors plays out in practice. Who are the competitors and how do they operate? How do they market themselves, and how do they differentiate themselves from each other?

- **Power of suppliers:** this is all about how much power the suppliers in the market have. This is determined by such things as the number and size of buyers and sellers in the market, and whether the market is regulated or not. A large seller in a market with few competitors is likely to have considerable power.

- **Power of buyers:** likewise, a large buyer in a market with many competing sellers is likely to have considerable power.

- **Threat of new entrants:** sometimes the competition is not from existing players in the market but from new entrants.

- **Threat of substitution:** sometimes the competition is not even from sellers of the same goods, but from sellers whose goods perform an equivalent function. For example, when Drinkalot package their fruit-juices they can put them in glass bottles, plastic bottles, plastic pouches or cans. A seller of cans, when selling to Drinkalot, would have to look beyond the can market for its competitors.

For example, Computalot could come up with the following analysis:

- **Market:** Computalot know the computer systems market quite well. There are many suppliers who can provide the hardware: the computers and printers; but there are far fewer who can put together a system, and then install and test it. When it comes down to suppliers who can supply the business analysis software and have the experience to offer consultancy to help Drinkalot gain a competitive edge through its use, there are to their knowledge only two other organisations; one of these can only provide business analysis software and consultancy, however, and not the computers.

- **Threat of substitution:** this is a possibility, as Drinkalot could buy the computers from one source, and install them and test them themselves. They could then buy business analysis software from another organisation and hire a separate consultant to give them the knowledge to get the most out of it. Such business analysis software is new, and those with the knowledge to use it are still scarce, so they might find this difficult.

- **Threat of new entrants:** on the other hand, there could be a number of consultants wanting to break into the market who are prepared to sell cheap (not in the sense of reduced prices, but in the sense of significantly more background hours) and learn on the job. Thus the threat of new entrants must be taken seriously.

WHERE DOES THE POWER LIE?

Who has the power, or at least perceptions about who has power, can affect the negotiation. Power is rather strange stuff and often has a bad connotation, since people immediately think of its use in a negative sense. The whole subject of power is explored further in appendix 4.

In practice, it is your perception of how much power you have that really counts, and you often have more power than you think. One reason for this is because you are very aware of your own weaknesses, but you try your best only to display your strengths. If the other party does the same, then all you see are their strengths and your weaknesses. The other party has weaknesses too, and it is your job to find these out as soon as possible.

In preparation for the negotiation, you should first think clearly about what power you have over the other party and what power they might have over you. Once you know this, then you can take action to increase your power and find ways to decrease that of the other party.

For example Computalot could make a power-analysis that runs as follows:

Sources of power are:

- **Expertise:** Computalot have general expertise in not only the supply of computer systems, but also in their installation and commissioning. They have special expertise in the application of the business analysis software.

- **Information:** they know their bid well and how it was put together. They have prepared well and are fairly certain they know who the competition is.

- **Having an alternative:** they do not have to sell this system at any price. They are a healthy and profitable organisation and if the overall gross margin on the sale is heading for less than 21%, they will not proceed with the negotiation. Instead they will walk away and concentrate their efforts on other prospects, one of which is currently looking very good.

- **Time:** they would like to close the deal before the end June as then they can then book the sale in the first half-year. This in fact lessens their power should the negotiation takes a long time.

- **Monopoly:** although they are not a monopoly in that they are not the sole supplier in the market, they are one of only three companies in the country who can supply the expertise to use the business analysis software.

They can increase their power as follows:

- **Preparation and fact-finding:** "knowledge is power", and Computalot should make sure they complete their preparation: analysing not just their own position, but trying to see how things look through the eyes of the other party.

- **Increase number of tradables:** the more they have to trade, the more power they have, as it gives them a greater chance of reaching a good agreement. They should brainstorm all the possibilities, be flexible, and be alert for new ideas.

- **Remove time constraint:** do they really need this sale in the first half-year results?

- **Have a better alternative:** they have a good alternative, but will need to align well to make sure they that they a) do not disclose this to Drinkalot, and b) make sure they stick to it. Things can look very different in the heat of the negotiation event.

- **Plan well:** they should create some scenarios in advance so they know what to do under all the likely circumstances. For example, what do they do if Drinkalot press them to supply the business analysis software and consultancy only?

WHAT HAVE YOU GOT TO NEGOTIATE WITH?

Negotiation involves trading, and to be able to trade you need to have something that you can give away in order to get something back. You also need to know when to trade and when not to trade, and what your alternatives to trading are. You should consider the following points:

- **Tradables:** these are quite simply the things you have to trade, and include price, delivery date and payment terms. There are a whole host of others too, depending on what is important to the deal. These could include, for example: a bonus for early installation; ownership of intellectual property; who is liable for what; and, who pays whom what in damages if things go wrong. A fuller list of possible tradables for a commercial negotiation is included in appendix 5, but it pays to brainstorm at this juncture to generate as many tradables as possible.

- **Cost, price and value:** a tradable will have some value to you that depends to some extent on cost and price, but can depend on other factors too. It is difficult to put a value on creative talent, for example, but it does have a value, and it helps to express this as objectively as possible. Each party of course is likely to attach a different value to each issue under negotiation.

- **Positions and interests:** there is a difference between what you actually want to achieve (your interests) and what you might offer on the journey to achieving these (your positions). Computalot's opening bid sets out a position from which they expect to move in the course of the negotiation. However, their need to have a signed deal by 30 June is a real interest.

- **"All prices are fictitious":** this is a helpful way of looking at the role of price in negotiation. Prices are fictitious because they represent positions and not interests; until the final deal is done they are not real prices.

- **Alternatives and BATNA:** alternatives are the steps you can take, should continuing the negotiation seem unlikely to bring you an acceptable result. Your BATNA is your Best Alternative to a Negotiated Agreement and a good BATNA can be very powerful. Computalot, for example, have already defined an overall BATNA: they will walk away if the deal does not generate a gross margin of 21%. This is realistic because they have at least one other good sales prospect within the timescale on which they would like to make a sale.

- **MDOs, LDOs and ZoMA:** because negotiation does not deal in right answers, for each issue you will have a range of acceptable positions: from an MDO (Most Desirable Outcome) to an LDO (Least Desirable Outcome). Computalot's MDOs will be set out in its opening bid and their LDOs represent the point at which they are prepared to use their BATNA. Drinkalot will likewise have an MDO and LDO for each issue, and the hope is that they will overlap, to give a ZoMA, a Zone of Mutual Agreement. For example, on payment terms, Computalot's MDO is 30 days and their LDO is 60 days, whereas Drinkalot's are 90 days and 60 days respectively. There is a very small ZoMA at 60 days.

These points are considered in more detail in appendix 5.

For example, Computalot could put together a list of tradables together with their value (initially only estimated as high, medium or low) to both themselves and Drinkalot. The list could be extended by adding LDOs, MDOs and BATNAs, and the result might look like this:

Tradable	Value	Value to Drinkalot (assumption)	MDO	LDO	BATNA
Price	Medium	High	£850,000	£750,000	Consider reducing if gross margin remains 21%
Delivery time	Low	Medium	12 weeks from order to commissioned	24 weeks from order to commissioned	If hold up due to Drinkalot, ensure it does not tie up own resources
Payment terms	High	Medium	30 days	60 days	Ask for stage payments giving more sooner
Stage payments	High	Medium	30-60-10	20-60-20	Ask for short payment terms
Gross margin	High	Low	30% plus	21%	Walk away
Expenses	Low	High – want to limit overall price	Expenses at cost	Capped (reasonable cap)	Increase price/resist discounting
IP ownership	High	Low	We own	We own	Walk away
Terms of trade	Medium	Medium	Computalot's or separate contract	Modified Drinkalot's	Involve legal function
Contract signing date	High	Medium	30 May	30 June	Challenge deadline internally

Tradable	Value	Value to Drinkalot (assumption)	MDO	LDO	BATNA
Initial consultancy	High	Medium	60 days plus	28 days	Walk away
Support and maintenance	High	High in short term, low in long term	5 years	3 years	Increase price/resist discounting
Relationship	High	High in short term, low in long term	100% chance of further business	50% chance of further business	Increase price/resist discounting
Drinkalot buy from various sources	Low	High if achieves low price	Gross margin of 40% plus	Gross margin of 30%	Walk away

WHEN WILL THE NEGOTIATION EVENT TAKE PLACE?

It is usually easy to set a time for the start of the negotiation event. In this case, Drinkalot have invited Computalot to a meeting, and the date for this has already been set. However, it is not so easy to say just how long the negotiation event will last, as this depends on how much money is at stake, how complex the issues to be resolved are, and just what difficulties are encountered during the event itself.

You should make an estimate, however. This will be valuable in managing deadlines and also in ensuring that there is enough time for any work to be done to ensure that the goods/services/works are ready to be delivered or received at the agreed time.

Your estimate can be based on past experience of similar negotiations or, if this is the first of a kind, then you should think through just might what happen and how long this might take. For example, will the opening meeting just be for you to present your bid, explain it and defend it, or will there be time for more? Will a second meeting be necessary for the buyer to respond to your bid with counter-offers and proposals, and will further meetings need to take place to discuss all the issues on the table and reach a conclusion? You should remember also to factor in time for the approvals process for both buyer and seller (should there be one), and for any last questions these might raise.

For example, Computalot could prepare as follows:

- **Length of negotiation:** the negotiation is estimated to take between three and four weeks as the value of the system is relatively high and there are quite a few tradables. It is likely that the first two meetings will consist mainly of presenting the bid and getting a response; the meat of the negotiation may take another meeting; and to get a final agreement yet one more.

- **Approvals:** getting approval should take no more than a further few days. On Computalot's side, the value falls within the authority limit of the sales manager. Drinkalot is a medium-sized private-sector company and, although this is a significant investment for them, alignment within the organisation appears to be good, and the managing director is likely to sign off the deal if the IT director and finance director both recommend it to him. There is a slight risk, however, that they might have to refer the deal to their new American parent, and this could add significant delay. This matter should be cleared up early during the first meeting, by asking Drinkalot just what their approval procedure will be.

- **Deadlines:** Computalot have a deadline to sign a contract by 30 June. They are not aware that Drinkalot are working to any real deadline; it has taken them a long time to get this far, and a few more months are probably not critical. Their existing system is still functioning and if pushed could be operated for another year or so.

WHERE WILL THE NEGOTIATION EVENT TAKE PLACE?

There are no hard and fast rules about where the negotiation event should take place. In some cultures it is the norm that the seller always travels to the buyer. On the other hand, some buyers believe that the disadvantage of travelling away is offset by the advantage of what can be learnt by seeing the sellers at home, and perhaps combining the negotiation meeting with a tour of their facilities. Sometimes travel practicalities dictate that a neutral venue – a hotel or conference centre – is used, or a seller might deliberately propose such a venue to avoid meeting at home where, perhaps, the factory is noticeably quiet and short of orders.

When travelling distances are great, audio- or video-conferencing can be used as an alternative to face-to-face meetings, but if it is at all possible the parties should meet at least once during the negotiation; there is so much to be gained by being able to interact with people personally. It can also be a good idea to take the opportunity to meet informally, where possibilities can be explored off-line in a more relaxed atmosphere.

In all cases, the following points should be considered:

- **Guests:** if you are hosting the meeting, then the other party are your guests and should be treated as such. They should not be kept waiting, and after a long journey they need a little time to recover.

- **Room:** this needs to be comfortable and large enough to hold everyone.

- **Seating:** it is traditional for the parties to sit opposite each other, despite what is said about this creating an adversarial feel to the proceedings. Practically, it prevents confidential information being read by a nosey neighbour from the other party, it gives people the comfort of being next to "friends" and it allows easier observation of the other party's reactions during the negotiation. In cases of joint problem solving, rather than negotiation, however, it is probably better to mix up the teams.

- **Facilities:** food and drink should be on hand and toilets nearby. Negotiation can be very tiring and involves a lot of talking, so water should be on the table.

- **Breaks:** most people work better in short bursts, with frequent breaks. You should plan in breaks beforehand, and if people seem tired and unable to concentrate, you should suggest an impromptu break, or an early finish followed by an evening session.

How do you want to conduct the negotiation? – Planning for the negotiation event

Once you have assembled as much information as you can in preparation for the negotiation event, you need to do some planning for the event itself. As part of your preparation, you will have made some assumptions about how things look from the other party's point of view, but of course you cannot be sure these are right. It pays, therefore, to be cautious when planning and not to plan too far ahead.

A good strategy would be to plan as far ahead as the end of the first meeting. During that meeting, you should learn a lot more, and this will enable you get together after the meeting, review progress, take a step back and plan further ahead. Depending on what happens at the first meeting, you may be able to extend your planning horizon beyond just one meeting ahead.

A plan is simply a means of getting from A to B. For example:

- **A is where Computalot is now:** they have made a bid for the accounting computer system.

- **B is where Computalot want to be:** they aim to sell the system to Drinkalot at the best possible price and achieve their objectives for time of agreement, price/gross margin, support/maintenance, relationship and consultancy days, as above.

And Computalot could come up with the following more detailed plan:

- **Overall plan (how to get from A to B):** negotiations start next week, are likely to last between three and four weeks, and may well be spread over four meetings. There is an internal deadline to complete the sale by 30 June: two months from now and six weeks from the date of the first meeting, giving a buffer of between two and three weeks. Planning ahead will only be done in detail to the end of the first meeting, and then progress will be reviewed before detailed planning takes place for the following meeting and beyond.

- **Short-term actions:**

  - Complete preparation: gather any final information needed to satisfy Kipling's six honest serving men.

  - Write down what has been prepared: document the preparation materials to allow them to be referred to for guidance during the negotiation event and to be updated as more is learnt as the negotiation proceeds.

  - Get the agenda for the first meeting: ask Drinkalot to send through such an agenda, together with directions on how to reach their offices and information on parking etc.

  - Do some preconditioning: at the same time as asking for the agenda, let Drinkalot know that there is significant demand for this type of system and a lot of interest in the business analysis software, where resource to implement it is scarce. (This is known as preconditioning, and will be covered later. The idea is to get Drinkalot thinking that they will be lucky to get the resource they need... and therefore they may have to be willing to close the deal quickly and/or pay a bit more).

- **At the first meeting, Computalot will:**

  ➢ Explain their bid, and in particular try to find out if Drinkalot are interested in any of the options they proposed.

  ➢ Try to find out where Drinkalot are coming from: are they just interested in price (as Computalot suspect), or are they genuinely interested in a top-class installation?

  ➢ Try to find out whether there is any internal tension that can be exploited between Drinkalot's buyer from their purchasing function and the user from the finance function.

  ➢ Defend their bid if necessary, and listen carefully to any proposals that Drinkalot make.

  ➢ Be careful not to disclose their 30 June deadline, or their gross margin target of 21%.

  ➢ Try to avoid getting into the heart of the negotiation, preferring to use the meeting as an information-sharing and fact-finding event. This gives them the chance to regroup and replan prior to a second meeting.

  ➢ Resist selling only the business analysis software and consultancy, as distinct from the complete system. If Drinkalot express a very strong preference to go down this route, however, Computalot would be prepared to do this for a price: in this case their objective would be to achieve an overall gross margin of 30%.

EPILOGUE

In this chapter you should have learnt all about the importance of preparation and just what it involves. In summary:

- Do your preparation, looking at things not only from your side but from the other side too.

- Do not forget that the other party will do its preparation too.

- Use Kipling's, "six honest serving men", as a guide to what questions need to be asked.

- Check your aims, and make sure your objectives are SMART.

- Align your own team, and find out as much as you can about the other party's.

- Check who has the authority to negotiate.

- Find out as much as you can about the market and the competition.

- Decide where the power balance lies, think of ways to increase your power, and remember that you always have more power than you think.

- List your tradables and assign a value to them, remembering that price has little to do with cost and that value can have little to do with price.

- Separate your interests from your positions.

- Remember that all prices are fictitious.

- Define your MDOs and LDOs and decide on your BATNAs.

- Do not forget the practical bits, such as where and when things take place, and how long they last.

- Be aware of any deadlines. If nothing else, working to a deadline decreases your power.

- Plan ahead as far as reasonably possible, and replan frequently.

CHAPTER 4

Attitude, behaviour, tactics and ploys – how to play the negotiation game well

INTRODUCTION

You've done your preparation, formed your team, know all about the other party and know what you have to negotiate with.

But just how are you going to conduct the negotiation? What attitude should you take and how should you behave? Just how will Drinkalot's team members behave and how will their personalities affect this behaviour in practice? At least you are dealing with an organisation in your own country, so you will not have to worry about too much about culture; but they do have an American parent.

Then there's tactics. You know your objectives and have some plans, but just what tactics should you use during the event itself to make sure your plan is a success and that you achieve your objectives? You've heard a lot about ploys and dirty tricks. How should you defend yourself against these and avoid falling into any traps?

Let's consider these points one by one.

ATTITUDE

The attitude with which you approach the negotiation will help to promote success. You should:

- **Have self-confidence:** self-confidence based on a sense of self-worth helps you to present your arguments in a convincing manner, where what you say is backed up by your body language.

- **Be assertive:** from self-confidence flows the ability to be assertive, neither aggressive nor passive, but able to confidently put forward your point of view while respecting that of the other party.

- **Not be swayed by perceptions of power:** as we have seen, power is a tricky thing. You should be clear where the power lies, and should not be swayed by attempts made by the other party to convince you that they have power over you when they haven't.

- **Not make assumptions:** if you have to make assumptions, then ask questions to check them at the first opportunity.

- **Be flexible:** flexibility is needed to be able to listen openly to what the other party is saying, to reflect on that, and then to modify your behaviour accordingly if necessary.

- **Be ambitious in your wants:** in general, those who aim high achieve more than those who do not.

- **Reframe how you see things:** trading always involves a gain and a loss, and it is easy to become attached to what you are about to lose, or to regret its loss afterwards. Try to see things in terms of what you have gained, rather than in terms of what you have lost.

- **Remain alert and watchful:** you should know now when to talk and when to be silent, when to say yes, when to say maybe, and when to say no; when to ask a question, and when to answer when asked. You need to be on the lookout for ploys.

- **Keep calm and carry on:** a good tactic for if the other party get aggressive or angry is just to keep calm and carry on as if nothing had happened.

- **Be aware of good manners:** nobody got a poorer deal by being courteous.

- **A good deal:** people like to feel they have a good deal, so you should make sure that the other party does. It could be said that the art of negotiation is to convince the other party that they have achieved a good deal by letting you have what you want.

BEHAVIOUR

A person's behaviour is all that we can see, hear or feel. Behind the way a person behaves lies a complex set of feelings, emotions, beliefs and values, known as personality. Personality is also affected by culture, and people from the same culture often display similar personality traits. This personality drives behaviour, but not necessarily in a logically consistent or even accountable way. When asked to explain why they behaved in a particular way, a person can find this hard to do and, even when they can offer an explanation, it sometimes makes little sense – even to themselves.

From a negotiator's point of view, behaviour is a reliable thing to deal with. Successful negotiating behaviours can be learnt, the behaviour of the other party can be readily observed, and this can consciously be taken into account to modify your own behaviour in the direction of success.

Negotiation is a universal process that works across personalities and across cultures. Whoever you are negotiating with, the negotiation game remains the same. You are simply dealing with different players.

THE THREE KEY BEHAVIOURS

One way of looking at how to play the negotiation game is to consider that there are basically three different behaviours that can be employed: aggressive, passive and trading. The model is simplistic and naturally each behaviour can be employed to varying degrees, but this approach remains nonetheless very useful.

There are two extreme behaviours:

- **Aggressive:** this is also known as streetwise behaviour. It is characterised by starting from a position of distrust, and is based on a desire to take all it can from the other party. The attitude is that of "all is fair in love and war". It is value-claiming in nature and seeks a win-lose outcome.

- **Passive:** this is also known as cooperative behaviour. It is characterised by starting from a position of trust, and is based on the belief that sharing and working closely together with the other party is the best way forward. The attitude is one of "love thy neighbour". It is value-creating in nature and seeks a win-win outcome.

Both styles have their problems. Aggressive, taking behaviour does not build strong relationships. Passive, sharing behaviour is open to abuse by aggression, manipulation and downright deception.

On the other hand, both styles have their place in negotiation depending on a) what sort of negotiation is under way: value claiming or value creating, and b) what is best needed at any particular time during the negotiation, in order to facilitate further discussion.

There is a third alternative to these extremes, however:

- **Trading:** This is also known as neutral behaviour. It is characterised by assuming distrust until trust is built, and is based on a belief that a) issues should be judged on their merits and b) trading is the best way forward, where nothing is given up unless something is received in return. The attitude is one of, "I'll trust you if you give me reasons for doing so". It is intrinsically neither value claiming nor value creating, but can be used to do both.

Trust is one of the key issues that determine which behaviour should be used when.

TRUST

Trust is an important issue, as it can drive behaviour. The problem with trust is that it involves an element of risk. If you trust someone, they can abuse that trust and take advantage of you. On the other hand, if you do not build trust then you will miss out on valuable opportunities to share information and collaborate to find solutions.

Trust needs to be built and then maintained. If you do not know much about the other party to the negotiation, then it is best to assume a position of no trust and proceed from there. Until trust has been built, you should make sure that you are minimising your exposure to being taken advantage of; you should think carefully about taking risks that require an "honest" response from the other party. Most deals involve an element of risk because they are based on an exchange of promises: "I will deliver these goods to you on Friday, if you pay me for them in four weeks' time." Here the seller is taking the risk: they must deliver on Friday but they will not get paid for another four weeks.

You should be careful how and where you invest your trust in business relationships. Even the best intentioned negotiators can sometimes not deliver on their promises, due to changing circumstances, lack of authority, office politics etc. And some negotiators are not even best intentioned.

A BEHAVIOURAL APPROACH TO NEGOTIATION

Taking a behavioural approach to negotiation has the big advantage that behaviour is observable, and having observed something you can react to it appropriately. Using the aggressive-passive-trading model of negotiating behaviour introduced above, it is possible to offer some basic suggestions about how to play the negotiation game as follows:

- **Observe behaviour:** observe the behaviour of the other party carefully. Are they behaving aggressively, using threats and trying to take, or are they behaving cooperatively and offering up information in response to reasonable questions?

- **Minimise the risks:** for example, if Computalot were selling to a foreign organisation they did not trust to pay on time, then they could reduce their risk by asking for some of the payment up front, or by delivering the goods in stages with each to be paid for before the next shipment, or they could insist that the buyer provide a third-party payment guarantee via a bank.

- **Build trust where appropriate:** make gestures yourself to build trust by behaving cooperatively. Where the negotiation is of a one-off nature and the parties are unlikely to meet again, then building trust is not really an issue.

- **Test the trust built:** use proposals and if-then questioning to test trust. "If you let us see your cost breakdown for this item, then we might be able to talk about price".

- **Behave appropriately:** where trust has yet to be built, use trading behaviour. Build trust by using passive, cooperative behaviour, and punish breaches of trust by using more aggressive behaviour.

- **Do not open with a passive move:** for example, if Computalot opens by saying, "we will agree to 60-day payment terms as a gesture of goodwill to get these negotiations started," this is open to an aggressive counter from Drinkalot that simply takes the 60 days and gives nothing in return. What's more, they could then sit there and wait for more "gifts"; goodwill does not come into it.

- **Use trading behaviour:** start from a position of assuming distrust and adopting trading behaviour. When dealing with the issue of payment terms, Computalot would have been advised to say, "our standard payment terms are 30-days but if you want to talk about increasing these, we would need to talk about a price increase."

- **Use passive, cooperative behaviour:** cooperative behaviour can be adopted in order to display the willingness to jointly share more information, invent options for expanding the pie and search for common ground. This will help to build trust.

- **Use aggressive behaviour:** adopting aggressive behaviour should be used with care and can be dangerous. It can be used to counter aggressive behaviour by the other party on the tit-for-tat premise that it will discourage further such behaviour. However, this can spiral out of control if aggressive behaviour is constantly met aggressively, and rapidly lead to destructive discussions, argument, conflict and ultimately deadlock.

- **When faced with consistently aggressive behaviour:** the best response is to use trading behaviour, reiterating the facts that a) you will get absolutely nothing from us unless and until we get something from you and b) we will try to judge each issue on its merits. This prevents naked taking but does allow issues (even if presented aggressively) to be explored. For example, when faced with what could be a spurious assertion of what the contract says, the contract should be examined in order to the judge the issue on its merits.

- **Separate the behaviour from the issue:** even if someone is behaving aggressively, it does not necessarily mean that the issues they are presenting have no merit. You should take time to separate the issues from the behaviour, and try to find ways to address them.

- **Remain emotionally neutral:** In all cases, you should try to remain dispassionate and emotionally neutral, and avoid attempts by the other party to elicit emotional responses. Human beings often make bad decisions, which they later regret, when powerful emotions are at play.

For more on a behavioural approach to negotiation see Kennedy's *The New Negotiating Edge* (Nicholas Brealey Publishing, 1998). In this book he introduces the terms red, blue and purple to stand for aggressive, passive and trading behaviours, and goes on to illustrate the power of this approach through the use of games such as Prisoner's Dilemma and the Red-Blue Game.

Behaviour is affected by a number of things: whether you are a buyer or a seller, personality, cultural background, emotional state, personal situation or just mood. The effects of personality and cultural background are worth exploring a little further, but you should take great care not to assume that because you know something about a person's personality or culture you can predict their behaviour.

PERSONALITY

Personality is hard to define. It is best understood by considering that you display a number of personality traits that predispose you to behave in certain ways. These traits mark you personally and as a whole make up your personality.

There are many tests that have been designed to measure a variety of personality traits, and psychologists would normally use a number of these in order to fully assess someone's personality.

Understanding personality certainly has its role in negotiation, but it also has its limitations. Its biggest use would be if you could accurately predict someone's behaviour from knowing his or her personality. This is not easy for a trained psychologist let alone for a commercial negotiator, and a little knowledge in this respect can be a dangerous thing. It is always better to observe behaviour and respond appropriately.

The impact of personality on negotiation is more fully explored in appendix 8.

CULTURE

Culture, like personality, can be hard to define, but can be understood simply as "the way we do things around here". Culture, like personality, influences behaviour. Negotiating with someone from a different cultural background, however, does not mean that you are playing a different negotiation game; it is the same game but played by someone with a rather different style. Humans are humans whatever their cultural background.

Knowing about culture, however, can significantly reduce the risk of being misunderstood and of giving offence. It prevents discussions becoming stalled and speeds up the whole negotiation process. As with personality, however, a little knowledge about culture can be a dangerous thing. It is always better to observe behaviour and respond appropriately and, if you need help, you should include a local person in your team.

The impact of culture on negotiation is more fully explored in appendix 9.

INFLUENCE AND PERSUASION

Influence and persuasion are separate skills, both aimed at changing someone's behaviour or point of view.

Influence is more of a broadcast activity, where you seek to change someone's behaviour by creating an impression of some sort, usually appealing to the emotions. For example, you can influence people by using a firm handshake or by making sure that you remember their name.

Persuasion is more directed at a specific situation or a specific person. You get your points across by building trust, developing a relationship, and then using well-reasoned arguments backed up with emotional appeal.

Both skills have their role in negotiation, and you should use your best to influence and persuade the other party to first understand your point of view and then have some sympathy for it. The more sympathy they have for your point of view, the more likely they are to concede more easily in negotiation. On the other hand, you should remain very aware of when you are being influenced and persuaded. Negotiation is primarily a trading activity, and you should be keenly aware that persuasive arguments such as, "it is only fair that we make a reasonable profit," are actually irrelevant. The counter here is, "yes, of course your organisation needs to make a profit, but please make it from other buyers, not from us." What is relevant here is to find out a) just what can be traded for a reduction in price and b) what alternatives the buyer has to buy elsewhere if the seller makes a stand on price.

Influence and persuasion have been written about extensively elsewhere. For a good introduction, see *Influence: The Psychology of Persuasion* (Harper Business, 2007) by Robert B. Cialdini.

FAIRNESS AND EQUALITY

Fairness is hard to define; it depends on one's point of view and is often confused with equality. It is valid however to ask the question, "is this fair and reasonable?" as long as these limitations are acknowledged. Something could be thought of as fair where it conforms to external norms against which it can be compared. Something could be thought of as unfair if it arises out of an abuse of power. However, it should be remembered that most negotiations are conducted on the basis of "what can we achieve?" rather than, "what is a fair solution?"

Fairness is not the same as equality. This can be seen by considering how the pie in a value claiming negotiation could be shared in a variety of different ways:

- **Equity:** outcomes should be based upon inputs – the person who made the pie gets more.

- **Equality:** regardless of the inputs, all get an equal share.

- **Power:** those with more authority, status, or control etc. should receive more than those in lower level positions.

- **Need:** those in greatest need should get more – the hungriest, or the thinnest.

- **Responsibility:** those who have acquired more should share with those who have less.

Equality can be defined, therefore, but fairness depends on what view you take. Very often in negotiations a party who makes a proposal and justifies it by saying it is fair, is simply taking a point of view in support of their proposal. Fairness is not a principle of nature but a construct of the human mind.

Whatever the difficulties in defining fair, however, or even in agreeing that fairness exists, humans do not like to feel that they have been unfairly treated and if proposals made during negotiation are seen as unfair, they may be rejected out of hand. If the final agreement reached is not perceived as fair, this might spoil the relationship and create an environment of unpleasantness that makes the agreement difficult to implement. An agreement perceived as unfair may be accepted in the shorter term but later come back to haunt you if the other party seeks revenge.

It is worth asking yourself the question, "how would I feel if this happened to me?" If you felt that it was unfair, then the other party probably would too.

WHERE A FAIR APPROACH CAN LEAD TO FAILURE

The following story related by Kennedy in *Managing Negotiations* (Business Books Ltd., 1980) is illuminating:

"A multinational corporation manufactured small domestic appliances in four European countries. All plants were of comparable size. Due to overcapacity it had been decided to reduce the manufacturing capability by 25%. The four national plant managers were called to a meeting to agree on this reduction.

The English management with their traditional sense of fair play came to the meeting with a problem-solving approach and failed to recognise the need to negotiate in this particular situation. "We feel that each plant should bear an equal share of the cuts. We have examined our operation and have identified areas which we could eliminate." The response was predictable: "We are interested to hear that your operation can be cut. We have looked at our plants and feel that each is a wholly integrated unit and not amenable to partial pruning."

The English factory was closed completely."

LEGITIMACY

Proposals should be given credibility where possible by reference to external norms, as this helps to promote the feeling of fairness. Power to extract the last cent from the deal should not be abused and on occasions it may be wise, usually for the sake of the relationship, not to use the full extent of one's power. This effect should not be overestimated, however, and it is an often-used ploy of salespeople to cry, "unfair," stress the need for a good relationship and therefore ask for better terms.

Returning to the issue of whether a seller's claim that they should, "make a reasonable profit out of the deal," the other question begged is: what does the word "reasonable" mean? Competition and the market will often dictate the amount of profit available, and this will vary from time to time, and from industry to industry, depending on market conditions.

However, humans do respond to words and concepts such as fair and reasonable, and a good challenge is to consider whether what you are discussing is indeed "fair and reasonable" by trying to find some objective criteria by which to judge what is fair and what is reasonable. It can help here to use the word "legitimacy" and ask:

- **Standards:** is there a neutral, external standard that defines the legitimacy of the issues under discussion or of any offers being made?

- **Custom and practice:** in the case of "reasonable profit", what is the industry average for this kind of market and what overall profit has the seller declared in their organisation's annual report?

- **Power:** where does the power lie? Is it being used legitimately, or is this an abuse of power?

COMMUNICATION

Effective communication in negotiation is essential. You need to be able to express your points of view clearly and understand easily those of the other party. A good questioning technique and good listening skills are required. Lack of effective communication leads only to misunderstandings, and significantly reduces the chances of a successful outcome to the negotiation.

In general, a skilled communicator will know the purpose of their communication and understand their audience (in this case the other party), as well as being able to speak clearly, ask good questions and listen carefully to the answers.

The whole topic of communication is covered in more detail in appendix 6.

BODY LANGUAGE

Non-verbal communication can take many forms, and these are often grouped under the heading of "body language", which has developed a life of its own as a separate subject.

A great deal of caution is needed, however. Extravagant claims about the power of body language are made but some of what is presented is just dressed-up common sense, and there are many myths concerning its use.

Humans by nature can "read" body language but as in all things some do this better than others. Equally, some humans are better at concealing the bodily expression of their thoughts and feelings than others. In negotiation you should certainly look for non-verbal communication, but should treat what you learn as assumptions and find ways of testing these. Similarly, you should be wary of giving away non-verbally what you do not wish the other party to know. The issue is similar to that of personality and a little knowledge can be dangerous.

The subject of body language is further explored in appendix 7.

TACTICS

During the preparation phase, you should have developed some strategic materials and plans to help you during the negotiation event itself. These would have included aims and objectives, market analysis, power analysis, tradables and alternatives (BATNA). In addition you should have made an informed best guess about the how the other party viewed these points.

Once the negotiation event itself is underway you will be using the three behaviours, as described above, to guide your conduct, but you also need to use good tactics in the heat of the event itself.

There are several points that need to be taken into account:

- **Set aside:** if you are making no progress on one issue, then you should suggest that it is set aside, to be considered later, when perhaps other things have come to light that may help.

- **Do not be afraid to adjourn:** if in doubt you should not just plough on, but instead ask for an adjournment. This can be used to check facts, get information or realign the team. Adjournments need not be long.

- **Use informal meetings:** informal meetings, often on a one-to-one basis, can allow people to express what they do not wish to say in public.

- **Use escalation:** escalation can be useful at times, where issues are referred to a higher level of authority. But you should be careful about using escalation too often, as it will reduce your authority and your credibility as a negotiator.

- **Use and recognise ploys:** ploys could also be called tricks, or traps, and are tactics used by one party to try to manipulate the other party in order to gain an advantage. Some are less ethical than others and are the stock in trade of an aggressive negotiator. They have their place though, and you need to learn both when to use them yourself and how to defend yourself against them. Ploys are considered in more detail below.

- **Use conditioning and preconditioning:** conditioning is all about setting expectations, and preconditioning simply means that you do this before the negotiation event takes place. The idea is to apply pressure to perhaps lower expectations. Drinkalot could indicate at the first meeting that budgets were tight because the new American parent had imposed a freeze while it reviewed the business worldwide; the implication being that Computalot would be well not to be too ambitious in their aims. This may well be true, but a) how frozen a freeze is, is always a debatable point, and b) in any case this is not really relevant to Computalot. Their task in the negotiation is to do as well as they can, leaving Drinkalot to sort out its own internal issues.

- **Try to avoid conflict:** if you get into conflict over an issue, then there is the temptation to descend into destructive argument, involving personal attacks, blaming and point-scoring. Such behaviour is best avoided, but if it happens then you should try to stop it quickly, by perhaps suggesting an adjournment, in order to allow the parties to cool off and make a more objective appraisal of the situation. Remember that disagreement is normal in negotiation, but conflict is not. Negotiation is in fact a technique to reach agreement without passing through conflict.

- **Try to avoid deadlock:** if you are deadlocked then there are a number of things that you could do to break out:

  ➤ Try even harder to see things from the other party's point of view.

  ➤ Take a helicopter view of the proceedings, viewing what's going on for what it is, not for how it appears to either you or the other party.

  ➤ Reframe the issue, and think about what you might gain by making a concession, rather than what you might lose.

  ➤ Try even harder to come up with some more tradables.

  ➤ Adjourn to reconsider in the quiet, away from the other party.

> ➤ Change the surroundings, by closing the meeting and agreeing to meet next at the other party's site.

> ➤ Use "off the record" one-to-one discussions to get to the real reasons behind the position the other party is taking.

> ➤ Escalate to higher levels of authority to see if they can remove obstacles by untying your hands on certain points.

> ➤ Change the negotiator(s) – there might simply be a clash of personalities.

However, you should not be overly concerned about deadlock. It happens, and if both parties really want to deal with each other, then a solution will usually be found.

- **Avoid making common mistakes:** there are a number of common mistakes in negotiation, and these are considered in more detail in appendix 10. You should review these now and vow to avoid them during the negotiation event itself.

- **Hostile negotiators:** every now and then you will encounter a tough, aggressive or downright hostile negotiator. The key here is to try to separate the issue from the behaviour, and then deal with the issue; again this can be more easily said than done. How to deal with hostile negotiators is also covered in more detail in appendix 10.

PLOYS

Ploys are tactics used by one party to a negotiation to manipulate the behaviour of the other party, in order to gain an advantage. They aim to coerce you to concede more. Whether they are ethical or not is often a matter of opinion, and depends to a large extent on culture, style, personality and situation. There are aggressive negotiators who genuinely believe the saying that, "all's fair in love and war," applies to negotiations. And there are passive negotiators who use ploys rarely, but do so more often when they are faced with aggression. The line between the use of legitimate persuasion, ploys and dirty tricks can be a fine one.

Ploys work by playing on the power relationship between the two parties. They aim to make you believe that you have less power than you have and that you should therefore settle for a lesser outcome. Perceptions of power are subject to all sorts of influences, very few of which are based on facts. Skilled users of ploys know this, and manipulate the situation and context to purport that their power over you is greater than it is. If you are not careful you can fall for this, believe you have less power and so lower your expectations. You have in effect ended up negotiating with yourself.

Defence against a ploy is logically quite simple, but in the heat of the negotiation event can be hard to come up with. Skilled users of ploys know this, and can exploit timing to perfection. Defence involves first recognising the ploy for what it is – a ploy, and then deciding consciously on how to respond: a ploy when identified becomes impotent. An accurate assessment of where the power actually lies and what alternatives you have is useful in these situations.

Things to think about are:

- **Use ploys with care:** if people feel they have been tricked, then this can leave a bad impression and weaken the relationship.

- **Decide if it's ethical:** before using a ploy. You can use a scale to help you, running from persuasion through conditioning, manipulation and coercion to force. You should also take into account the situation, as what is ethical in one situation may not be in another.

- **Recognise ploys as they are played:** you should recognise a ploy at the time it is played against you, assess your options and respond appropriately.

- **Name the ploy with care:** it can be useful to name the ploy to the other party as they play it. This has the advantage of stopping its effect, but can have the disadvantage of implying that the other party is acting unfairly. This can worsen the relationship for no good gain. In addition, if you are wrong and what has been presented is not a ploy then this can be embarrassing.

- **Counter the ploy:** make sure you know in advance how to counter the common ploys. If in doubt, you should ask for an adjournment to consider how to respond.

Here is a brief list of some of the more common ploys, together with suggestions on how to counter them:

- **Intimidation:** psychologically destabilising the other party by sitting close, leaning across the table, sitting in a bigger chair, positioning them with the sun in their eyes. A lesser form of this is hosting the negotiation in circumstances that ooze wealth and power, either at the organisation's prestigious headquarters or at an up-market hotel. In countering this: you should ask to be made comfortable; you should not let the bad bits upset you; and, you should enjoy the good feeling of life in a nice hotel.

- **Preconditions:** the idea is that either you meet these preconditions and comply, or there is no purpose in continuing to the negotiating event. Preconditions can include insistence on "buyer's contract only", "assignment of intellectual property rights", "prohibitions on working for competitors" etc. In making your response, you need to decide: whether the other party really has the power to insist on these or not (and some large organisations do); whether the issues are really of value to you; and, how much do you want to negotiate with someone who insists on such preconditions? As an alternative to saying either yes or no, you can always try to trade at this point, by asking, "are you prepared to consider a higher price, if we agree not to work for the competition for six months?"

- **Non-negotiables:** these are similar to preconditions but played later, during the negotiation event, and you should make a similar response. In addition you could ask, "why is that non-negotiable?" or, "who says so?" A reasoned argument has more power than a naked assertion. In the extreme, and to make a point, you could always come up with non-negotiables of your own.

- **Deliberate misunderstanding:** the other party deliberately misunderstands a point to their advantage, in the hope that you miss it or are too timid to correct it. This often manifests itself as an incorrect summary. You should respond by checking all summaries etc. and challenging any points you feel are not being presented as they were discussed.

- **Good cop, bad cop:** this is often played between end user (good cop) and professional buyer (bad cop) with the idea that that the good cop gets incremental concessions, to get the sale or to maintain the relationship, as a result of bad cop's behaviour. The response should be to point out that you are getting mixed messages, and insist that the other party present a united front.

- **Grinding down:** this is the continuous repetition of the same demand regardless of the response unless it is "yes". It is played in the hope that you will be ground down by the other party and make a concession just to avoid the pressure. To counter this, you should make it very clear after a number of repetitions that you are prepared only to trade, in respect of that particular point, perhaps making or repeating a reasonable proposal. If the behaviour continues then you should consider stopping the negotiation.

- **Belittling a proposal:** for example, the other party reacts incredulously to a proposal with, "you can't be serious, that's nowhere near realistic." In response you could say, "that's what I'm prepared to offer at the moment, maybe if we move on and explore other possibilities that will help."

- **Pickpocketing:** this involves deliberately taking a little extra post agreement. For example, by paying late or by changing the specification. This should be met by identifying the problem and raising it with the other party. You could say, "I don't know if you're aware, but you're paying in 60 days rather than the 30 we agreed. If this continues much longer we shall have to raise our prices by 2%."

- **Salami:** the other party seeks to slice the agreement up and negotiate separately on each issue to its advantage. For example, "let's agree on payment terms first, how about 60 days?" If you proceed like this, then you'll lose the ability to trade across variables and indeed to trade at all. You should insist that issues need to be linked and that you need to talk about the whole deal. You should remember that, "nothing is negotiated until everything is negotiated."

- **Last minute nibble:** after a lot of hard work, the agreement is almost ready to be signed. You have agreed on price earlier, but the buyer suddenly says, "if you could just let me have a final discount of 5%, then I'm sure we can get this approved straight away and sign now." This is deliberately played when you have invested so much in getting a deal and are at your most vulnerable. Remember, in defence, that you have three choices: yes, no and trade. The ploy can be met by saying, "I thought we'd agreed on price, but if you want to open the discussion again, we're happy to do that." This is in fact a nicely put "no". An alternative would be to propose a trade (maybe one that was declined before) as follows, "if you bought maintenance for five years, then we could accept the 5% price reduction."

- **Lacking authority:** after ostensibly reaching agreement, the other party says they will have to refer this to their boss, who then asks for more concessions. You should always ask your opposite number early on in the negotiation whether they have the authority to negotiate as this makes the ploy far harder to play.

- **Highballing:** the other party makes unreasonable demands. The problem is that if you allow these to be made, even if you do not accept them, they can then be used as a marker against which the outcome is judged. It is better to challenge the demand as soon as you recognise it to be unreasonable, by saying, "my information seems different from yours, can we just check that we're talking about the same thing." Here is where thorough preparation pays off: in this case you will have an idea whether a price, for example, is widely out of line with the market.

- **Deadlocks and deadlines:** the other party can deliberately deadlock the negotiation; refusing to continue until a certain concession is made, knowing that time is important to you. On the other hand they might insist, "we need to complete the deal by Friday at 5.00 pm," and ask for concessions to help this to be met. In both cases, you should challenge the deadline as it is getting in the way of the outcome.

- **The Bogey:** this is the name Karrass (see below) gives to the technique of saying, "I love your product, but sorry I just can't afford it," or, "sorry, but I've only got X amount in the budget." This is followed by a request to lower the price. This can be met by challenging the budget and asking, "if you really do like my product more than anyone else's, then aren't you prepared to pay more for it?" or by asking who needs to be involved to remove the budget restriction, or simply by having ways to reduce the specification to fit the price.

- **Final Offer – take it or leave it:** this is sometimes played early in the negotiation in order to force a quick concession. It runs the risk of course that you will leave it if you have a good alternative. If you haven't, or if you think it's a bluff, then you might be better saying, "it's a bit early to talk about final offers, we haven't even talked about some of the issues yet."

- **Lowballing:** to some extent this is the opposite of highballing. The idea is to offer something at a very low price, but perhaps something that does not contain what you want. When the price of the necessary add-ons is included, the price is not low at all. The idea is to get to the table with the expectation of a low price. To counter this, you should always check that what is on offer is what you have asked for before you begin to negotiate. If it is not, then you should ask for a revised proposal at the start.

- **Sell cheap – get famous:** this is often used to tempt you to reduce your price in return for a way in to a large organisation where there will be repeat business, or in return for a big-name reference. The problem is that once you have sold cheap, then it's very hard to raise your prices later. If there is genuinely scope for repeat business, then you could make an offer based on volume-related discounts. If a big-name reference has real value to you then you could regard this as a fair trade and accept.

If you want to know more about tactics, ploys and dirty tricks then Jonathan O'Brien presents a good summary in chapter 11 of his book *Negotiation for Purchasing Professionals* (Kogan Page, 2013), and Charles Karrass provides a comprehensive list in alphabetical order in his book *Give and Take: The Complete Guide to Negotiating Strategies and Tactics* (Harper Business, 1993).

Epilogue

In this chapter you should have learnt all about how to play the negotiation game well: how to have the right attitude and use the right behaviours; how to communicate and persuade; what tactics to use; and, how to defend yourself against ploys. In summary:

- Be confident, have a positive attitude and aim high; negotiators who aim high achieve more.

- Observe the other party's behaviour and react appropriately.

- Remember the three behaviours: aggressive, passive and trading.

- Use the right behaviour at the right time.

- Proceed with caution when trust has not yet been built, and build trust when it is right to do so.

- Personality and culture influence behaviour, but don't overdo it here, it's behaviour that counts.

- Use influence and persuasion to guide the other party towards your point of view.

- Don't worry too much about what is fair, but do look for ways to support your arguments by legitimate comparisons with external standards.

- Put effort into good communication, making sure you are understood, asking questions and listening to the answers.

- Observe body language, but do not set much store by it unless it is in conflict with what the person is saying.

- Use a wide range of tactics to suit the situation.

- Watch out for ploys, tricks and traps, and avoid making simple mistakes in the heat of the moment.

- Make sure you know how to handle hostile negotiators.

CHAPTER 5

The negotiation process

INTRODUCTION

You've done your preparation, learnt some theory and gone on to understand how best to play the negotiation game by behaving appropriately during the negotiation event itself. You've seen how personalities and culture could influence the way that Drinkalot behave, and you've also been primed to look out for the ploys and dirty tricks that they could use during the event to influence things in their favour.

How then will the event unfold? Does it have some structure and are there any rules? How will you reach a successful agreement?

Let's consider these points one by one:

NEGOTIATION AS A UNIVERSAL PROCESS

Negotiation is a universal process that operates across cultures and across the personalities involved in the negotiation itself. There are many different ways of representing the process but typically it can be drawn as below, and consists of four steps, preceded by a preparation phase. On the left is the formal process with named steps; on the right is the same diagram, but this time instead of each step being named, there is a brief description of what happens during that step.

The process is drawn as a straight line, but in practice negotiation can be a non-linear and highly iterative: steps are not completed before the negotiation moves on, returns are made to previous steps to complete unfinished business, something new crops up or something becomes undone.

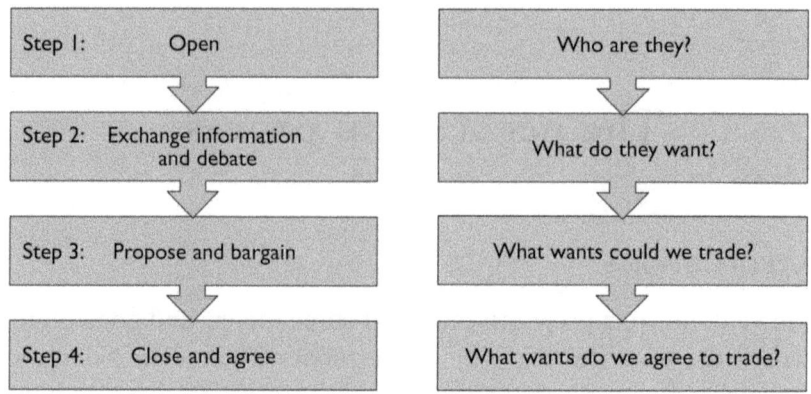

Diagram 4 – The negotiation process

Step 1: Open

INTRODUCTION

The purpose of this step is for the parties to meet each other, introduce themselves and size each other up, as a way of beginning the negotiation. This is also a time to agree on agenda, timescales, breaks and other housekeeping matters. How long this all takes is often culturally determined. However, you should not rush things; it is an opportunity to get a feel for the other party before the negotiating event starts, and it is also a chance to relax slightly and make sure that you are calm.

Then, when both parties are ready, the negotiation event itself should be started.

OPENING THE NEGOTIATION

What happens during this first step is very important as it can set the scene for later. In commercial negotiations the seller is very likely to have already made an opening bid as part of a bidding process, and this will form the basis of the opening discussions.

In this case, Drinkalot, as hosts, would open the talking and thank Computalot for coming to the meeting. They might explain that the meeting's purpose is to clarify some uncertainties in Computalot's bid and to discuss possibilities going forward. This is suitably vague: it shows definite interest in negotiating with Computalot, but does not imply that Computalot are the only bidder.

Step 2: Exchange information and debate

INTRODUCTION

The purpose of this step is to give the parties the opportunity to share information about their positions, interests and alternatives, or indeed about anything else. You have a chance to find out from the other party what they want and why, and you should use this step to a) fill in the information gaps left over from the preparation phase, and to b) replace assumptions and educated guesses with facts. Important information you will want to find out from the other party includes:

- The issues that will need to be negotiated.

- Their take on these issues: the interests behind their positions (the why, behind the what).

- Their LDO and MDO.

- Their BATNA.

Of course the other party is likely to be trying to find out this kind of information from you too, and depending on the type of negotiation and the style in which it is being conducted, you may or may not wish to reveal this.

In the one extreme of a value-creating negotiation between parties with a high degree of trust that focuses on achieving a win-win outcome, then it is probably best to be very open and reveal all. The discussion will then focus on brainstorming to create options and tradables, and the negotiation will proceed more like a joint problem-solving session. In the other extreme of a value-claiming negotiation between parties with very little trust, and where the party adopts an aggressive style, then you are probably best to reveal little and concentrate on finding out as much as you can. Most commercial negotiations lie between these extremes and you should proceed cautiously at first, but be prepared to share more when some trust has been built.

CONSTRUCTIVE DEBATE

This step proceeds best by adopting the principles of constructive debate. These include the use of:

- **Neutral statements:** a neutral statement is one made by one party which simply informs the other of their views, opinions, attitudes and approach towards the matter under discussion. The statement is neutral in that it does not contain attacks, assertions or threats, and the manner in which the statement made is matter of fact. For example, when dealing with a complaint, "we have checked the records and, yes, the goods were delivered six weeks late," is a neutral statement of fact.

- **Assurances:** these are used to keep the debate open and positive, and to motivate the other party to do the same. For example Drinkalot could say, "we've heard about your expertise in business analysis and are keen to explore this further."

- **Questions:** for example, Computalot could start with some open questions such as, "how do you feel about the fruit-juice market this year?" These are generally used to further debate. Or they could start with some closed questions (which can generally be answered by yes or no) such as, "is this specification for the computers up to date?" These are generally used to check assumptions or to ascertain facts. This is your chance to ask lots of questions, and you should use it now to find out what you do not know.

- **Summaries:** these are useful to both check for understanding and show the other party that you have indeed been listening carefully to what they are saying. For example, Drinkalot could say "before we go any further, we would just like to check that you feel a price rise of 5% per year for maintenance and support is appropriate." A summary should be so phrased that it does not imply agreement and if necessary this should be clarified, "we would just like to make it clear, however, that we will need to come back to this point later, as this was not within our range of expectations."

- **Signals:** these show willingness to move, but do not commit to anything at all specific. For example, Computalot could say, "you have asked for a price reduction of 25% overall but we must stress that this kind of reduction is not possible." This is a signal that movement is possible on the point of price, as the words "this kind of reduction" are used. Whereas, if Computalot had said, "you have asked for a price reduction of 25% overall but we must stress that a price reduction is not possible," this is a clear signal that no movement on price is possible.

The opposite of constructive debate is destructive debate. This is characterised by using language that irritates the other party, attacking or blaming the other party, scoring points, interrupting the other party, blocking off lines of discussion, making assertions about the other party's behaviour, and by the use of threats. When on the receiving end of such destructive behaviour, it is easy to retaliate in kind. This just makes the situation worse, however, and the negotiation is likely to slide into deadlock and disaster. The best response is to avoid emotional entanglement and counter destructive debate with the principles of constructive debate.

You should remember that disagreement is normal at this stage in the negotiation. The point of playing the negotiation game is to move from a position of disagreement to one of agreement, and in this step you are only just starting to explore how this might be done.

BEHAVIOUR

Important behaviours to think about during this step are:

- **Build trust:** remember that building trust can take time. As noted earlier, it is better to assume no trust at the beginning and proceed from here cautiously. If you are too trusting at the start you can be taken advantage of.

- **Ask questions and listen to the answers:** ask lots of questions, and try to find out as much as you can. Listen carefully to the answers and use these to fill in the gaps in your knowledge. You should remember that the other party does not have to answer your question; their answer might not be telling you the full truth either, or it might be a bluff. You need to listen not only to the verbal answer but also to the tone of voice, and you need to observe the body language and the behaviour of other members of that party's team.

- **Do not answer your own questions:** let the other party do the answering, and do not feel that silence needs to be filled.

- **Do not weaken a strong argument by propping it up with a lot of weak ones:** the weak ones will be easy for the other party to counter, and this will reduce the credibility of your case, irrespective of whether you have a strong argument or not.

- **Do not say too much:** by doing so you can inadvertently give away information you do not want to. Silence can be a useful tool as it invites the other party to fill it.

- **Think carefully what information you want to divulge:** do not withhold information, however, without a good reason, as this can mislead the other party and ultimately get in the way of finding agreement.

- **Set aside difficult issues:** if it becomes apparent that some issues are going to be difficult, then they should be parked for further discussion later. Maybe they will become easier to handle as the negotiation proceeds.

MOVING INTO THE HEART OF THE NEGOTIATION

At some point the exchanging of information and debate must come to an end. There are no clear rules about how long this will take, but it often becomes apparent that it is time to move on when it is felt that all the issues have been surfaced, both parties have run out of positive things to say and questions to ask, and that the discussion is going round in circles or even sliding into destructive debate.

To prevent this from happening, you should keep this step as short as possible; moving forward, you should feel that you have gathered enough information to start to explore what agreement might look like. The negotiation process does not run in a straight line, remember, and you can always return to this step later, in order to find out more.

Step 3: Propose and bargain (the heart of the negotiation)

INTRODUCTION

In order to proceed to agreement, there needs to be movement by each party, and at the end of the last step each party had the chance to signal to the other where movement might be possible. The purpose of this step is first to explore what movement is possible by making tentative proposals and then, once the responses to these have been discussed, to confirm what movement is possible by striking definite bargains that satisfy both parties.

This step is all about trading – the golden principle of negotiation: if you give me this, then I will give you that. What you are prepared to trade are your tradables, and when you trade these you talk about trading concessions. If you simply make a concession without getting anything in return, then strictly speaking you are not negotiating, you are simply saying "yes," and you are wasting the opportunity to trade that concession for something that you want.

PROPOSALS

Suppose Drinkalot had signalled that they were prepared to move on payment terms by saying, "our standard payment terms are 90 days." (This is a signal because it does not say at all, "we can only accept payment terms of 90 days," and it invites discussion of under what circumstances other non-standard payment terms could be agreed.)

The next stage would be to tentatively explore this point further and Computalot could make what is known as a proposal, "if you were to decrease your payment terms, we would be prepared to talk about reducing our price." This is nothing firm and fixed but it takes the process of moving towards agreement a step further.

Finally, and usually after considerable further discussion, the proposal might be converted into what is known as a bargain, "if you decrease your payment terms to 30 days, then we will reduce our price by 2%." This is firm and fixed and if the answer is yes, then a bargain has been struck and agreement has been reached, on this point at least.

When making proposals the following points should be taken into consideration:

• **Language:** the language of a proposal should be tight, formal and assertive, so that there is no misunderstanding, no beating about the bush and no room for misinterpretation. Phrases such as, "I wish...", or, "it would be nice if...", should be replaced by, "I need...", or "it is necessary that...".

- **Clarity:** you should present the proposal clearly and succinctly: without justifications, unjustified assertions, amusing anecdotes etc.

- **Conditional:** a proposal should consist of a condition and an offer, and be in the form of, "if you do this for me," (the condition), "then I will do this for you," (the offer). It is best to put the, "if you do this for me," condition first as this has more impact on the other party. If you make the offer first it can imply acceptance without the condition.

- **Do not be too specific:** a proposal is a tentative suggestion about how to move forward and should invite a response which both allows the proposal to be discussed further and gives you the opportunity to find out more about where the other party is coming from. The condition can be (but does not need to be) specific, but the offer should always be vague.

For example, if Computalot proposed, "if you buy some maintenance in advance, we might be prepared to reduce the price," the condition is vague and the offer is vague. If they said, "if you buy maintenance for three years in advance, we might be prepared to reduce our price," the condition is now specific, but the offer remains rightly vague. Both of the above are good proposals; which one Computalot should use will depend on the exact situation during the negotiation.

- **Do not make unilateral concessions:** you should always make conditional proposals and not fall into the trap of making a concession as a sign of goodwill. It invites the response of, "thank you for that," and the attitude of I will wait for more.

- **Look to make proposals that trade across issues:** you should take advantage of the fact that each party may value things differently and therefore will be prepared to trade something of lower value to itself for something of higher value. For example, Computalot do not value the printers very highly as they are inexpensive items they sell virtually at cost. They do value maintenance highly, though, and would like Drinkalot to buy as much as possible. They might propose to trade free printers for extra maintenance.

- **Get all the issues on the table:** you should not start to make proposals until you feel that all the issues have been surfaced during the previous step. You should treat the negotiation as a whole, involving all issues, even if you make proposals dealing with only one at a time. Tie all your proposals together into a package.

- **Silence:** once the proposal has been made, you should be silent and wait for a response from the other party.

RESPONSE TO PROPOSALS

A good proposal will always have a vague offer as we have seen: "if you were to decrease your payment terms, we would be prepared to talk about reducing our price." This invites a question as a response, and Drinkalot could ask, "how big a reduction are you talking about?" to tempt Computalot to be more specific.

It is by this process of making and responding to proposals that each party learns what the other party is prepared to accept. The potential points of agreement are revealed in much the same way as the continents were discovered. They were always there, just waiting for someone to come along and "discover" them.

When considering how to respond to proposals, the following should be borne in mind:

- **Listen:** you can learn a lot by listening carefully to the response the other party makes to your proposals and to the proposals the other party makes. It is reasonable to assume that they value highly a) what trades they ask for and b) what they will only trade for a high "price". For example, if Drinkalot open aggressively on price, say by asking for a 25% discount across the board, it is fair to assume that price is important to them.

- **Interests and not positions:** as proposals are made and responded to, you should steadily try to build a better picture of the interests that lie behind the other party's positions. As you do this, it should become clearer where common ground lies. For example, Computalot need to find out is why price seems to be so important. Is it because Drinkalot's buyer needs to get savings or is it because budgets are genuinely tight?

- **Ask questions:** by its very nature a proposal is a vague offer. You should ask questions to make the offer less vague. For example, if Drinkalot proposed, "if you would accept less money up front, we could reduce our demand for a 25% price reduction," Computalot might ask, "what sort of reduction are you talking about?"

- **Do not interrupt:** people do not like being interrupted. And in any case, even if what is being proposed is of no interest (or in the extreme is rather offensive), you can still learn something from what listening to what is on offer.

- **Do not be in a hurry to say "no":** people find having "no" said to them discouraging. And even if the proposal really does not interest you, you can still learn from what is on offer by asking questions. It may be too, that on further reflection, or in combination with other proposals, it becomes possible to respond more positively.

- **Encourage the other party to make more proposals:** it is only by listening to their proposals that you can really find out where the other party is coming from. If the other party does not make proposals, then finding an agreement is going to be difficult.

For example, if Drinkalot made almost no proposals, beyond perhaps, proposing a price reduction Computalot could encourage them by asking, "what do you think about the maintenance; is our five year option of interest to you?"

You should keep a list of both parties' proposals and their answers, and review this at regular intervals. You should compare it with the list of tradables you developed during the preparation phase and update this as more and more information is revealed. This will help you to see further possibilities for proposals and promising routes to agreement.

LINKING

There are sometimes advantages to linking several issues together in a proposal. For example, Computalot could propose, "if you buy an extra computer now (to cope with your projected increase in business) and if you buy the business analysis software for it and if you commit to a further 30 days of consultancy next year, we would be prepared to offer a discount on the computers of 5%, based on the quoted price, provided we receive the order within the next two weeks."

They are offering to discount something they make little money on (computers) in return for selling more of something they make more money on (business analysis software and consultancy) and at the same time sell some volume before the end of the half-year.

WHAT HAPPENS WHEN IT ONLY BOILS DOWN TO PRICE?

It is far easier to make proposals and ultimately strike bargains if there are many things to trade off against each other. Where there is only one tradable, for example, price, each party is likely to fight hard for its own interest, which is unlikely to match that of the other party.

Building trust, asking questions and sharing a bit more information will all encourage the development of further options to trade. Sometimes, however, it is just not possible to do this. There could genuinely only be one tradable or you may be faced with an aggressive party who believes that cooperation will only lead to a loss for them and who tries to force concessions on a limited set of tradables solely for their own advantage. In this case, the pie is fixed and the outcome can well be a win-lose, a lose-win or even a lose-lose. Relationships can suffer and there is plenty of scope for the abuse of power. Where there is only one tradable, or maybe only one or two, then you need to think particularly carefully about the following points:

- **BATNA:** be aware of what your alternatives are and be prepared to walk away from agreements that will be worse than your BATNA.

- **Legitimacy:** is there anything you can do to legitimise your position in order to make it more sellable to the other party. For example, when asking for a price rise, can you justify it on the verifiable grounds that your raw material prices have gone up out of your control?

- **Power:** you should not abuse any power you have to force an agreement on your terms. If the other party tries to force an agreement on you, and you really have no alternative but to accept, then if you feel that you are being taken advantage of you should say so.

  You could perhaps also point to times in the past when you have helped the other party in times of need, and stress all the advantages that come with a good relationship. If all this fails, then you should restrict customer service to an acceptable minimum, offer no favours in the ongoing relationship and find a new organisation to trade with as soon as you can.

- **Relationship:** you should take into account what migh happen to the relationship if you do force an agreement on your terms, or if one or both parties come to regret the deal struck in hindsight.

In fact, with just one tradable there is nothing to trade, just concessions to be made by each party to the other, and if an agreement is reached, then it may well rest on the BATNA of each party rather than on anything else.

For example, suppose Drinkalot came back to Computalot in three years' time and asked to buy another two computers to expand the system to meet the needs of their expanding organisation. Computalot might propose a price of £100,000. To which Drinkalot might say they were only prepared to pay £60,000. If Computalot have a walk-away BATNA at their LDO of £90,000 (the price at which they break even on the computers) and Drinkalot have a walk-away BATNA at their LDO of £80,000 (the price at which they can buy from a dealer down the road), then the BATNAs win, and Drinkalot buy from elsewhere.

In arriving at their BATNAs, however, both parties would have had to weigh up the pros and cons. Computalot would have taken into account the lost revenue on further maintenance, but perhaps also the gained revenue on any help Drinkalot would need to integrate the computers into the existing system. Drinkalot would have taken into account the extra cost of integrating the computers. Computalot would have been advised too, to think about the consequences of allowing the system to slip from their grasp, so to speak, and Drinkalot could have welcomed the opportunity to wrench Computalot's hold on the system from them.

BARGAINS

Proposals push the negotiation further towards agreement by asking for a concession (the condition) in return for something (the offer). However, although the condition may be specific, the offer is still rather vague. A bargain on the other hand is a clear and specific statement with a request for a specific concession, in return for which something specific is on offer.

For example, if Computalot have already proposed, "if you buy some maintenance in advance, we might be prepared to reduce the price," and got the reply, "Ok, but what are you talking about here?" then they could proceed with the clear and specific statement, "if you buy five years' maintenance in advance, we could discount the maintenance price by 10%." This is a bargain, but note that it has not yet been agreed.

The flow of the negotiation is therefore from:

- **Signals,** which state what wants we might consider trading. For example, Drinkalot's signal of, "our standard payment terms are 90 days," makes it clear that under the right conditions, they would be prepared to trade a reduction in payment terms for something.

to

- **Proposals,** which state what wants we would trade if we can get the right "price" for them. For example, Computalot could reply, "we understand that, but if you were to decrease your payment terms, we would be prepared to talk about reducing our price." This is a proposal.

to

- **Bargains,** which state exactly what wants we will trade under what conditions. For example, when asked by Drinkalot just what they had in mind, Computalot could reply, "if you decrease your payment terms to 30 days, then we will reduce our price by 2%." This is a bargain.

  A Bargain is still not an agreement. To be so, it requires an explicit "yes" from the other party. Drinkalot could agree, in which case a bargain has been struck on this point. Or they could ask, "could you still give us a 2% discount if we reduced our terms to 60 days?"

to

- **Agreements,** which state exactly what wants have been traded for what. For example, the discussion could continue a little and finally end up with Computalot summarising, "great, we just want to check what we've agreed to here. You will pay us in 60 days, for which we will give you an overall price reduction of 1%." Agreement has been reached on this issue.

On the point of maintenance, Drinkalot could take Computalot's offer of a 10% price reduction for five years' up-front commitment and after some further discussion offer the bargain of, "if you give us a 5% discount on the maintenance price, we will commit to three years' maintenance now, but we will pay yearly in advance." To which Computalot might respond, "if you want to pay annually, then we will increase the price by the rate of inflation each year." And if Drinkalot now say, "ok," then agreement has been reached, this time on the issue of maintenance.

A negotiation will naturally flow from signals to proposals to bargains as more and more questions are asked and answered, more and more information is exchanged, and more and more ideas emerge about what kind of final agreement there is to be made.

In order to get from a bargain to an agreement there may be yet further questions and clarifications. A bargain invites the same sort of response as a proposal, and the same things should be borne in mind. The difference here, however, is that you should be striking bargains from a position of the knowledge gained by passing through the earlier steps of the negotiation process and not from the position of ignorance that could well have prevailed at the start of the negotiation. Thus you should not jump to bargains too early; only moving there when a final solution seems close and when you feel that what you offered will be subject to minor adjustments only.

In practice, however, where for all sorts of reasons the earlier steps of the process might not have been executed as well as they could have been, there is ample scope for surprises. In this case there is no other alternative but to return to earlier steps in the negotiation to seek more information, clarify issues and revise proposals.

CONCESSIONS

In order to move to agreement, concessions have to be traded and the question naturally arises about how big these concessions should be. There is no easy answer to this, as it depends very much on the circumstances. The following points should be borne in mind:

- **In general, concessions should be small and get smaller:** if you make big concessions, this can imply that your starting position was unreasonably high, losing you credibility and therefore bargaining power. You will be asked for more, particularly if you give the concession easily. For example, when faced with Drinkalot's request for a 25% price reduction, Computalot should certainly not be tempted to consider anything like this. Instead, they could avoid the issue by replying, "it's a bit early to talk about the overall price yet, let's talk about something else first; we have a few questions...."

- **The more you know, the easier it is to make the right concession:** and if you are unsure, you can always ask for more information. A lack of information can be a real problem when what is being talked about is new or different, or has not been bought or sold much before. Here, you should resist the temptation to simply bargain from a position of ignorance, and thus end up splitting the difference (see below) between two different opinions. Instead, you should look for comparable instances, try to understand why the other party holds their opinion and, if appropriate, let the other party know why you hold yours.

- **The other party should work hard to get a concession:** if concessions are given easily, then again it can imply that your starting position was unreasonable. Also, if the other party feels they have had to work hard to get agreement, they are more likely to feel that they have got a good agreement and be happy with the outcome of the negotiation.

- **Don't say yes too quickly (even if you like the bargain on offer):** if concessions are offered easily, then it is possible that there is more to come. By saying yes too quickly you will not be able to take advantage of this. For example, suppose Computalot responded to Drinkalot's request for a 25% price reduction by offering 10% coupled with a request for payment terms of 60 days. Then, even if this had been Drinkalot's real aim (their interests on price and payment terms) they would be better to press for more. The concession was offered easily (and therefore it was easy to give), implying that there is more to come, which although it might not be so easy to get, is well worth pursuing. Drinkalot could say, "thank you for that, but we really do need to achieve the 25%. Perhaps we should talk about some other issues first, before returning to price."

- **Be careful as deadlines approach:** deadlines bring stress, and with stress comes the temptation to concede in order to meet the deadline. You should ask yourself just why there is a deadline, who imposed it and whether you can do anything about it, before rushing to concede.

- **Don't just split the difference:** there is no good reason to do this unless the difference is very small, you stand to lose very little by a split and the goodwill generated outweighs this loss in any case. Instead, you should challenge any request to split the difference by asking why this is the best thing to do. For example, suppose after a lengthy discussion Computalot had offered a price reduction of 5% as a result of a number of trades. Drinkalot might then return to the matter of price and suggest that a reduction of 15% was reasonable on the grounds that it was half way between their position of 25% and Computalot's of 5%. Computalot could challenge this by saying, "we understand where you are coming from, but it's just not like that. This is a big, complex job for us and 5% is as far as we can go."

NOTHING IS AGREED UNTIL EVERYTHING IS AGREED

There is a saying in negotiation that, "nothing is agreed until everything is agreed."

This means that, although you might reach agreement on issues one by one, the process is one of first exposing all the issues, then making proposals for all the issues and then converting these into bargains and agreements. Although what you have at the end is a set of these sub-agreements, one for each issue, they are part of a deal that has been negotiated as a whole. And it is the whole deal that must be agreed.

For example, suppose Computalot and Drinkalot have (among other things) agreed the following:

- Payment terms: 60 days.
  1% discount on overall quoted price.

- Stage payments as follows:
  20% on order placement, 60% on system installation, 20% on completion of testing.

- Maintenance: 3 years' commitment.
  10% discount on maintenance price.
  Paid yearly in advance.
  Amount to be paid is quoted price adjusted by rate of inflation as measured by the UK Consumer Price Index.

- Consultancy: 40 working days.
  5% discount on quoted consultancy price.
  Discount preserved for additional days ordered within one year of signing agreement.

And then Drinkalot (having been instructed by their American parent) asks to retract the payment term concession from 90 to 60 days, saying that they are prepared to lose the 1% discount, Computalot could point out that this would affect the whole deal as their offer of 1% took into account other things that were on the table. They could say for example, "if you could also agree to go back to the quoted stage payments, then we would accept this."

There is a well-known ploy, often used by buyers, called "salami", which aims to cut the deal into thin slices, an issue at a time, and reach agreement on these separately. The idea is twofold, first of all it prevents changes to one issue affecting the whole deal, as above, and secondly it allows the buyer to reduce the seller's room for manoeuvre. For example, if Computalot allowed the deal to be salamied, then each issue would be discussed from beginning to end and agreed in turn. Drinkalot could try to pick off everything except price and then ask for an overall discount. Computalot, having nothing left to trade, might then find they have to concede more than they wanted to without being able to get anything in return.

Step 4: Close and agree

INTRODUCTION

At some stage, it is in one or both parties' interest to end the bargaining and to close the negotiation with an agreement, and this is the purpose of this step. This closure is critical as there can be significant pressure at this stage, making it easy to make unnecessary concessions in order to reach a final agreement.

There are two important considerations about closing a negotiation: how to close and when to close, and these are considered in turn.

HOW TO CLOSE

The following techniques are often used to close the deal:

- **Summary close:** a summary is made of all that has been agreed up to now, highlighting the concessions you have already made and emphasising the value of the deal currently on the table. For example, Computalot and Drinkalot could for one last time simply run quickly through all the points agreed, and confirm that these do indeed form the deal.

- **Concession close:** a final concession is offered, coupled with the willingness to close. For example, as they run through the points of the deal, Drinkalot could hesitate or start to reopen discussions. Computalot might judge it appropriate (because they want a deal before the end of the first half-year and time is running out) to say, "if you can agree now to what's on the table, what we've just run through, then we could offer you a further discount of 2% on the total price."

- **Adjournment close:** an adjournment is suggested during which the other party is asked to consider their position and accept the deal on the table. It is often used after an attempt at a summary close or concession close and puts further pressure on the other party. Computalot could say, "look, that's a good deal. Why don't we take a break so you can consider it in private? We've been going round in circles for the last few hours and we really can't keep on like this. Let's meet back in here in twenty minutes. What do you think?"

- **Or else close:** the offer to close is accompanied by the threat of a sanction if closure on the terms on the table is not achieved. The threat must be credible and must be carried out if the offer to close is not accepted. This can be used to put even more pressure on the other party should other attempts to close fail. For example, Computalot (who are fed up with Drinkalot just asking for more and more discount) could say, "look, we've told you repeatedly that we've nothing more to give you on price. We're sorry, but if you cannot agree to the deal on the table now, we'll pack up and go home." This close should clearly be used with care.

WHEN TO CLOSE

Deciding when to close can be difficult and is often a matter of judgment. On the one hand there is pressure to prolong the negotiation in order to gain the most from the other party, while on the other hand there is pressure to conclude the negotiation to stop the other party gaining even more. It is certainly too early to close if you make a final offer which is rejected, forcing you to continue the negotiation. It is certainly too late if you are being forced into accepting concessions that could have been avoided. The process proceeds best as follows:

- **Signal readiness to close:** a party shows its readiness to close by using signals to indicate that it wants to reach agreement. For example, Computalot could say, "well, that's it then; is there anything else we need to discuss?"

- **Attempt closure:** when things seem ready, a trial close is used to sound out the other party. The close is carefully phrased and a way out is provided, such that if the trial fails the negotiation can be reopened with no problems for either party. For example, Drinkalot could reply, "no, but let's run through all the issues for one last time, just to make sure we haven't missed out anything."

- **Move steadily and surely to close:** a close should not be rushed; it can be tempting when closure seems so near to jump to the end too quickly. Using time pressure can be effective, but it can also backfire if the other party feels rushed and therefore forced to agree.

- **Agree any final details:** any last (small) details should be agreed. "Small" details not resolved have a habit of blowing up later. For example, suppose that Computalot and Drinkalot had not agreed on how long it would take Computalot to put an engineer on site to fix a computer should it break down. Then, given that Drinkalot use the computers 24 hours a day every day of the week, the difference between Drinkalot's view (that 4 hours is reasonable) and Computalot's (that 24 hours, working days only, is reasonable) could lead to an unfortunate dispute if a computer broke down on a Friday evening and could only be repaired the following Monday.

- **Summarise the deal:** the deal should be run through with the other party in its entirety, in order to ensure that nothing has been missed and nothing has been misinterpreted.

- **Handle final objections and doubts:** the realization of impending closure can cause people to panic in case they have forgotten something. This may manifest itself as the sudden appearance of objections and other reasons why the deal should not be completed at this time. You should always take objections seriously and handle them calmly.

- **Get stakeholder buy-in:** in the euphoria of closing the deal, it is easy to forget that it is often being negotiated on behalf of someone else. The various stakeholders need to be fully bought in and each party may need time to consult with them before the deal can finally be closed.

- **Handle last-minute ploys:** when closing a deal you can become emotionally very vulnerable; the end is in sight and the temptation to relax concentration is high. In addition, there is often a degree of personal commitment to achieving the final deal that can outweigh professional judgement. Under such circumstances you can fall prey much more easily to last minute ploys, such as that of being asked for one last concession just as the deal is to be signed.

- **Shake hands:** shaking hands can be a very effective thing to do at the point of agreement. It symbolizes the closure, and is such a powerful social symbol in many different cultures that the other party will think harder about backing out after a handshake.

- **Get approval:** formal approval is often needed for both parties, and time should be allowed for this to take place. You should be careful here, because, if the other party is not fully authorised to do the deal, then formal approval is not just going to be a formality. You might find yourself in the situation that the approving body says no, or more likely asks for this and that further concession. In this case the negotiation will need to be reopened. Of course, the other party could be using a ploy here and this could be just another way of extracting a last minute concession.

- **Confirm the agreement in writing:** The final step of closure is to confirm the agreement in writing, in order to secure clarity and prevent the deal from coming undone later. In commercial negotiation the written agreement is often in the form of a contract.

EPILOGUE

In this chapter you should have learnt all about the negotiation process and its four distinct steps. In summary:

- Negotiation follows a universal process, independent of personality and culture.

- This process consists of four steps: Open, Exchange Information and Debate, Propose and Bargain, Close and Agree.

- Avoid accepting the first offer.

- Never just concede, always try to trade.

- Use good positive constructive behaviour during debate.

- Always use the if... then (condition... offer) construct when making proposals.

- Put the "if you do this...," before the, "we will do that..."

- Move from signals to proposals, to bargains to agreement.

- Remember that, "nothing is agreed until everything is agreed."

- Close the whole negotiation at the right time and in the right way.

- Write down what has been agreed as soon as possible.

CHAPTER 6

What happens next?

INTRODUCTION

You've done the deal and are happy with it. The negotiation took time and had been tough: Drinkalot applied a lot pressure on price. However, by standing your ground and emphasising the overall value of the system to Drinkalot, you managed to achieve your objectives. You feel that A. Buyer was a little disappointed as they had quite possibly not fully achieved their savings targets, but that A. User felt good in that the budget could be stretched to cover what delivered some very powerful business analysis capability.

So, you've done your bit. But just what needs to happen next to make sure that the computer system is implemented well, and that Drinkalot get the value from the business analysis that you've promised. How will that summary you signed off on at the end of the negotiation get converted into a contract? Hadn't you better carry out a review too, to learn for the future?

And what about the implementation? Are both your organisation and Drinkalot's fully committed to making this work? Will you have a role in what happens next? And just how is your organisation going to cope with the all that change that you feel sure will come?

Let's consider these points one by one.

WRITING DOWN THE AGREEMENT

This should be done as soon as possible after agreement is reached, and you should either a) jointly write a summary during the last step of the negotiation process and sign it together with the other party there and then, or b) ensure that one party writes a summary shortly after the closing of the negotiation event and sends this to the other party for agreement and signature.

CONTRACTING

Contracting is the art of transforming the agreement into a contract. How this is best done depends on the value, complexity and type of goods/services/works being bought and sold. You should aim to write the shortest possible contract, compatible with these considerations; writing and agreeing long contracts costs time, money (lawyers) and frustration.

The type of contract can also depend on the law under which the commercial transaction takes place. There is a fundamental difference between the basis of law in the USA and the UK on the one hand, and most of continental Europe on the other hand. In Europe, the law itself says much more about what happens if nothing specific is agreed, and this is often acceptable to both parties. In the USA and the UK, however, the law dictates much less, and so contracts are generally longer.

There is also a cultural difference at work. In the USA and UK, detailed contracts are the norm, and the implied view is that we will distrust you so we need to write everything into a contract. In some countries, and where the value of relationship is prized, a long contract's implication of distrust can appear insulting, particularly if a pro-forma contract is produced early on, before the parties have had time to get to know each other.

In simple cases, it may be that you have agreed to trade using the standard terms and conditions of purchase of the buyer, with one or two exceptions. In this case a purchase order could be written, setting out the commercial terms as agreed and then referencing the standard terms and conditions. For example the order from Drinkalot could read, "this purchase order is placed in accordance with our standard terms and conditions of purchase (copy attached) with the following exceptions..." At the other extreme, when complex high-value items are being bought and sold, a full contract might be necessary, negotiated with the support of lawyers.

It is sometimes the case that agreement is first reached on commercial terms, and then a second negotiation follows on the legal details. This has the advantage of speed, as it allows work to start, but the disadvantage that you are starting work without a fully signed contract. What you do here depends on the risk you are taking and whether you can easily protect yourself against this or not.

Once the contract is signed, the original should be filed somewhere safe, leaving working copies for everyday use.

INTERNAL REVIEW

It is always good practice to get the team together and review the negotiation. You should leave a short time for reflection, before the review takes place, but not too long. People have a habit of not being available and of forgetting things as time goes by.

Questions to ask yourself during the review include:

- How do you feel about the negotiation and its outcome?

- How do you think the other party feels?

- Can you objectively measure the outcome? And if so, have you done better or worse than before?

- What did you do well? And what did you do not so well?

- How can you improve for the future?

COMMITMENT

At the end of the negotiation, when agreement has been reached, both parties must commit themselves to implementation in the timescales agreed. This can sometimes present problems, due to the complexity of what needs to be implemented, for example, or if some stakeholders have not been bought in to what is going on. When constructing the final agreement you should therefore always bear in mind that it should be SMART (Specific, Measurable, Achievable, Realistic and Time-constrained):

- **Specific:** is it completely clear just what needs to be delivered and under what commercial terms and conditions?

- **Measurable:** can you measure how successful the implementation of the agreement is? In simple agreements for the supply of goods, this could involve monitoring how well delivery dates have been met and how many failures there are due to quality issues. For more complex agreements involving the supply of services you should put in place a "service level agreement" with KPIs (Key Performance Indicators) to monitor performance against agreed targets.

- **Achievable:** is what has been agreed achievable? There is no point on agreeing something that cannot be achieved in practice. For example, if you agree to pay in ten days, can your finance function actually do this? Are the KPIs achievable? Computalot and Drinkalot could foolishly agree that the computers had a target uptime of 99%, forgetting that the computers were new models, delivered complete with teething trouble that reduced the uptime to less than 90%.

- **Realistic:** is the agreement realistic for both parties, in the sense that it can be implemented in accordance with the agreed timescales without causing huge issues? If not, it will rapidly come undone, despite what was agreed.

- **Time constrained:** have delivery dates and implementation schedules been agreed?

It is rare in commercial agreements to find that one party has in fact been negotiating in bad faith; in other words they have no intention of implementing the agreement. However, it can be that a party needs some reminding or some help, where some parts of their organisation who are affected by the agreement were not involved or even informed about it, and who do not feel obliged to implement it. This can happen, for example, when a global agreement is reached with a single supplier that cuts right across existing country arrangements.

In fact, any change of supplier is likely to increase uncertainty, increase workload and cause issues, and this should always be borne in mind. Depending on scope and complexity, the implementation should be viewed as an exercise in change management. An interesting perspective is given on this from the sales point of view by Sharon Drew Morgen in her book *Dirty Little Secrets* (Morgen Publishing, 2009).

It also helps to regard the agreement as a living agreement. Issues are likely to arise during its lifetime, as markets, people and circumstances change. These must be discussed and resolved by further negotiation, rather than simply being ignored.

IMPLEMENTATION

The implementation itself is not usually the responsibility of the teams that negotiated the agreement. However, it is the responsibility of those teams to ensure that everything is in place to allow the implementation to go smoothly.

Steps that can smooth the path of implementation include:

- **Understand what implementation means:** is this simply substituting one stationery supplier for another, or does it mean that disruptive building work needs to be done, new processes have to be implemented and people have to change jobs? In the case of Drinkalot, they certainly have to think about all these issues when installing the new computer system, and what about the time it will take to transfer over the data from the old to the new system?

- **Ensure both buyer and seller are involved:** both parties need to think about the implications of the implementation. In this case, Computalot are responsible for the installation of the system itself, before testing it jointly with Drinkalot and then handing it over to Drinkalot to use.

- **Plan in advance:** once you know what is required, you should put plans in place to inform people what will happen, to write the new procedures, to train staff, to prepare the area for the installation works, to test the new system to your requirements etc. etc.

- **Involve the right people:** you should ensure you know who the stakeholders are, and inform or involve them at an early stage. It can be a good idea to involve the implementation team in the latter stages of the negotiation, in order to avoid the agreement simply being "thrown over the wall".

- **Manage the ongoing relationship:** if implementation involves the provision of services, then it is not just a one-off event. Depending on the nature of the services and the length of contract, then service-provision needs to be managed on both sides.

Drinkalot will need to make sure that someone in their finance function is responsible for the day-to-day management of the new computer system, and Computalot will need to make sure that they have in place the right team too. This will include not only management of the help-desk services, but also the provision of a contact person responsible for ensuring that the use of the business analysis software is a success. In addition, both parties would be advised to have regular (three-monthly to begin with) formal commercial reviews, involving Computalot's sales function and Drinkalot's purchasing function, to check that all is going well.

CHANGE

Change is inevitable and needs to be successfully navigated; the effects of change need to be managed. A lot can happen in the future that might affect Computalot and Drinkalot's agreement. For example:

- The business analysis software does not give Drinkalot the benefits that they had foreseen.

- Computalot go bankrupt and cannot carry out their obligations to maintain the system.

- The new high-speed computers never achieve the required reliability.

- Drinkalot's new American owner decides to standardise on one financial system worldwide, thus rendering Drinkalot's new investment useless.

- Drinkalot gets a new procurement director who reviews consultancy and maintenance fees across the organisation and decides that they must be renegotiated.

And so on... the list is endless.

It is good practice to carry out a risk analysis prior to agreement, to identify risks and put in place contingency plans if necessary, particularly if you are dealing with high-risk items. Drinkalot should certainly do this in this case, because they cannot run their everyday accounting without the system; the system is critical to the performance of the organisation as a whole.

On the other hand, you cannot plan for the unknown and you need to be flexible to deal with whatever happens in a constructive way, which often means further negotiation.

In practice, change may well throw up items that could lead to disputes over the contract between Computalot and Drinkalot. If the new computers do not perform, for example, Drinkalot could say that Computalot had failed to deliver reliable computers. But Computalot would be wise to check that the cause of this was in fact the computers themselves, and not, for example, a temperature or power-stability problem, before trying to find an acceptable solution. This might lead to a dispute that needs to be resolved – by patience, flexibility and... more negotiation.

EPILOGUE

In this chapter you should have learnt a little about what happens after the negotiation itself ends, and how you can take some early actions to help make this a success. In summary:

- Write down the agreement as soon as it has been made and get both parties' agreement.

- Change an informal agreement into a formal purchase order or contract as soon as possible.

- Keep your contracts simple.

- Carry out an internal review, to learn from the experience, so that you can perform better in the future.

- Make your agreement SMART, so that everyone feels committed to implementing it.

- Plan for implementation in advance.

- Make sure the right people are in place to manage the implementation and the ongoing relationship.

- Be prepared for change; plan contingencies in advance and remain flexible.

- Be prepared to continually renegotiate the contract.

CHAPTER 7

Negotiation in a nutshell

Negotiation is a game, and as with all games you need to know how to play it well. Here is a short summary of how to do this:

GENERAL

- Be clear what negotiation is – a tool for solving certain kinds of problems.

- Consider the alternatives and decide whether negotiation is the right approach to solve your problem. It is usually (but not always) the best way of deciding the terms and conditions of a commercial relationship.

- Remember:

  - Negotiation works by trading something you have for something you want.

  - The negotiation game has relatively few rules and no real winners or losers.

  - It is a game, however, that follows a definite process.

  - And, there is definitely a best way to play it.

- Aim high.

- Do your preparation.

- Improve your communication skills.

- Understand the three styles of negotiation: aggressive, passive and trading...

- ... and focus on trading.

- Understand the four-step negotiation process:

  ➤ Step 1: Open.

  ➤ Step 2: Exchange information and debate.

  ➤ Step 3: Propose and bargain.

  ➤ Step 4: Close and agree.

- Do not worry too much about win-win and win-lose – your aim is to get as much as you can.

- Remember, though, to consider not only the outcome but also the relationship.

- Measure the outcome of a negotiation objectively if possible, and try to understand whether you did better than last time.

BEFORE THE NEGOTIATION

- **Seller:** put in a good bid that is attractive, ambitious, realistic and defendable.

- **Buyer:** know what you want to buy and review the bids using objective criteria.

- **Buyers and sellers:** learn about each other.

Preparation

- When doing your preparation, always try to look at things from the other party's point of view as well as your own.

- Check your aims, and make sure your objectives are SMART.

- Align your own team, and find out as much as you can about the other party's.

- Find out as much as you can about the market and the competition.

- Decide where the power balance lies, think of ways to increase your power, and remember that you always have more power than you think.

- List your tradables and assign a value to them, remembering that price has little to do with cost and that value can have little to do with price.

- Separate your interests (what you really want) from your positions (the means of getting there).

- Have a BATNA – a Best Alternative to a Negotiated Agreement.

- Plan ahead as far as reasonably possible, and replan frequently.

Tactics

- Observe the other party's behaviour and react appropriately, using the right behaviour at the right time.

- Proceed carefully when trust has not yet been built, and build trust when it is right to do so.

- Personality and culture influence behaviour, but it is behaviour that counts.

- Use influence and persuasion to guide the other party towards your point of view.

- Don't worry too much about what is fair, but do look for ways to support your arguments by legitimate comparisons with external standards.

- Observe body language, but do not set much store by it unless it is in conflict with what the person is saying.

- Set aside difficult issues for later discussion, and adjourn when necessary in order to seek more information, consider your options, or realign the team.

- Watch out for ploys, tricks and traps, and avoid making simple mistakes in the heat of the moment.

- Make sure you know how to handle hostile negotiators.

STEP 1: OPEN

- Let both parties set the scene.

- Clearly state your opening position.

STEP 2: EXCHANGE INFORMATION AND DEBATE

- Ask plenty of questions.

- Listen carefully.

- Understand the other party's viewpoint.

- Test your assumptions by asking questions.

- Summarise to check for understanding.

- Use signals to show what you might be prepared to trade.

STEP 3: PROPOSE AND BARGAIN

- Brainstorm to create more tradables if necessary.

- Try to trade something that has a low value to you for something that has a high value to you, remembering that what has a low value to you may have a high value to the other party.

- Make proposals using the, "**if** you do this…, **then** we will do that," format.

- To begin with do not be too specific with your proposals.

- Steadily become more specific and convert proposals into bargains by making concessions.

- Never make unilateral concessions – always get something in return – and never accept the first offer.

- Make your concessions small and hard to get.

- Legitimise your bargains if possible, by appeal to precedent or higher authority.

- Move from signals to proposals, to bargains to agreement.

- Link all your bargains into a final package – nothing is agreed until everything is agreed.

STEP 4: CLOSE AND AGREE

- Know when to close.

- Know how to close, and use the appropriate method.

- Hold you nerve and look out for last minute tricks.

- Summarise what has been finally agreed and get agreement from the other party.

- Write down what has been agreed as soon as possible.

AFTER THE NEGOTIATION

- Change an informal agreement into a formal purchase order or contract as soon as possible.

- Keep your contracts simple.

- Carry out an internal review, to learn from the experience, so that you can perform better in the future.

- Make your agreement SMART, so that everyone feels committed to implementing it.

- Make sure the right people are in place to manage the implementation and the ongoing relationship.

- Change happens – be prepared to continually renegotiate the contract.

APPENDIX 1

Further reading and resources

SALES AND PROCUREMENT

Building Excellence in Strategic Procurement Management, by Steve Mallaband and Ros Howard
Grosvenor House Publishing, 2014
ISBN: 978-1-78148-683-2

Dirty Little Secrets, by Sharon Drew Morgen
Morgen Publishing, Austin Texas, 2009
ISBN: 0-9643553-9-6

SPIN-selling, by Neil Rackham
Gower Publishing Ltd., new edition, 1995
ISBN-10: 0566076896
ISBN-13: 978-0566076893

NEGOTIATION

Getting to Yes, by Roger Fisher and William Ury
Penguin Books, second edition, 1991
ISBN: 0-14-015735-2

Give and Take: The Complete Guide to Negotiating Strategies and Tactics, by Chester L Karrass
Harper Business, revised edition, 1993
ISBN: 0-88730-606-3

Managing Negotiations, by Gavin Kennedy, John Benson and John McMillan
Business Books Ltd. (an imprint of the Hutchinson Publishing Group), 1980
ISBN: 0-09-141580-2

Negotiating Commercial Contracts, by David L Sheridan
McGraw-Hill Book Company (UK) Ltd., 1991
ISBN: 0-07-707348-7

Negotiation for Purchasing Professionals, by Jonathan O'Brien
Kogan Page Ltd., 2013
ISBN: 978-0-7494-6771-5

Negotiation: Process, Tactics, Theory, by David Churchman
University Press of America, second edition, 1995
ISBN-10: 0819199478
ISBN-13: 978-0819199478

Negotiate the Best Deal, by Gerald Atkinson
Director Books, 1990
ISBN: 1-870555-74-0 (paperback)
ISBN: 1-870555-19-8 (hardback)

The New Negotiating Edge, by Gavin Kennedy
Nicholas Brealey Publishing, first edition, 1998
ISBN-10: 1857882059
ISBN-13: 978-1857882056

Win-Win? by Andrew Cox
Earlsgate Press, 2004
ISBN: 1-873439-22-9

COMMUNICATION

Body Language: How to Know What's Really Being Said, by James
Borg Pearson, third edition, 2013
ISBN-10: 1292004517
ISBN-13: 978-1292004518

Body Language: Common Myths and How to Use it Effectively,
by Dr. Alex Drewnicky
Available on web via standard search

Building Excellence in Business Communication, by Ros Howard and Steve Mallaband
Grosvenor House Publishing, planned early 2015

Effective Communication: The Most Important Management Skill of All, by John Adair
Pan, unabridged edition, 2009
ISBN-10: 0330504266
ISBN-13: 978-0330504263

PERSONALITY

The Social Psychology of Bargaining and Negotiation, by Jeffrey Z Rubin and Bert R Brown
Academic Press Inc., 1975
ISBN-10: 0126012504
ISBN-13: 978-0126012507

CULTURE

Global Negotiation: The New Rules, by John Graham and William Hernández Requejo
Palgrave Macmillan, 2008
ISBN-10: 140398493X
ISBN-13: 978-1403984937

Riding the Waves of Culture: Understanding Diversity in Global Business, by Fons Trompenaars and Charles Hampden-Turner
Nicholas Brealey Publishing, third edition, 2012
ISBN-10: 1904838383
ISBN-13: 978-1904838388

INFLUENCE AND PERSUASION

Influence: The Psychology of Persuasion, by Robert B. Cialdini
Harper Business, revised edition, 2007
ISBN-10: 006124189X
ISBN-13: 978-0061241895

ONLINE RESOURCES

CIPS (Chartered Institute of Purchasing and Supply)
www.CIPS.org
CIPS is a membership organisation but lots of information is available to non-members under the headings: Knowledge and Bookshop.

Program on Negotiation at Harvard Law School
www.pon.harvard.edu
Free reports are available on certain topics. The monthly "Negotiation Briefing" covers a wide range of topics in an easy-to-understand format, and is worth subscribing to.

The Thomas-Kilmann Conflict Mode Instrument (TKI)
www.kilmanndiagnostics.com

APPENDIX 2

Buying and selling

INTRODUCTION

"Procurement is about satisfying a need by buying the right goods and services, at the right time, at the right quality and at the right price."

"Sales is about satisfying demand by getting the right product to the right person at the right time and for the right price."

These definitions are typical of those found in the literature, and of those used in many organisations with purchasing and sales functions. You should notice the careful use of the word "right", which signifies that there is a trade-off to be had between specification (how many bells and whistles), quality, delivery-time and price. You should also note the difference in emphasis of procurement on "need" and of sales on "demand". Professional buyers make a very clear distinction between needs and wants, whereas salespeople like to satisfy demand... which can often be wants.

Within many organisations there are well-established policies and procedures that govern how things are bought and how things are sold. There are also purchasing (also known as procurement, sourcing or buying) functions and sales functions. The performance of these functions is measured, as is that of the buyers and sellers who make them up. The buyers and sellers are trained in a certain way, and are often financially incentivised to perform well by the use of personal, team and company bonuses. Procurement follows a definite process, as does sales, and it is worth investing time to learn about these.

These policies and procedures, these processes, this training, and the way in which performance is measured and rewarded have a great deal in common across all organisations. And they all lead to buyers and sellers having certain, but different, mindsets, which they bring to commercial negotiations.

There are distinct differences between what drives a buyer and what drives a seller, and this leads to different behaviours that can be hard to understand. In general, buyers are driven by need to get the best price, deliver savings and sign a binding contract, whereas sellers are driven by the need to get the sale, meet their sales target and invoice as much as possible.

When negotiating, knowledge of how the other party is likely to think can be very valuable. It enables you to see the problem from the other party's point of view and better understand what is of value to the other party and what is not.

Points to consider are:

- **Behaviour of buyers:** as a seller, understanding how a buyer might be thinking will help you negotiate better.

- **Behaviour of sellers:** likewise, as a buyer, understanding how a seller might be thinking will be helpful.

- **The procurement process:** as a seller, understanding the buying process (what is driving the buyer) will help you to negotiate better.

- **The sales process:** likewise, as a buyer, understanding the selling process (what is driving the seller) will be helpful.

These are dealt with one by one in this appendix.

Behaviour of Buyers

A professional buyer, however, is more likely to behave as follows. They will:

- Believe that a) competition is good and drives down prices, b) only rarely are single-source "selection" procedures the right way to go and c) time should always be invested to find alternatives and thus competition.

- Believe that if the purchasing function has not been involved in this area of buying before, then there are significant savings to be made.

- Have a strong desire to be involved at the beginning of the process – if not then the business can give away negotiating headroom (by disclosing budgets) or intellectual property, etc. In extreme instances, business partners have been known to approach a buyer with a done deal and ask them to "negotiate the price".

- Be driven by the need to get savings in support of targets to get a bonus.

- Concentrate on the deal at the expense of the relationship – from experience they know that relationship in business deals can be overrated.

- Concentrate on buying to fulfil needs and not wants.

- Believe that price has often very little to do with cost – it is set by the market and by the supplier's situation at the time of purchase.

- Believe that suppliers do not have to make a profit on each and every deal – they only have to make an overall profit to stay in business – and they should make this on someone else's deal.

- Insist on buying on price where all else is truly equal and suppliers have been pre-qualified as fit to supply.

- Concentrate on the facts and demand precision in specifications, deliverables, pricing and documentation of agreements.

- Be driven by process, rather than by personality. Processes tend to be more onerous in the public sector, rather than in the private sector.

- Distrust partnerships and long-term deals – things change fast in business and such things can be difficult to get out of. In addition, they can create unhealthy dependency in both directions.

- Have difficulties with the quality of the relationship with their own business – in many organisations the procurement function still struggles to convince its business colleagues that it can add value, and is viewed as adding delay and only being interested in price.

- Insist that a formal purchase order should be written for everything bought (with reference to a matching contract). This ensures the visibility of all spends and highlights opportunities for further involvement of the purchasing function.

BEHAVIOUR OF SELLERS

A good salesperson is likely to exhibit the following behaviour. They will:

- Try to lock out the competition, by getting in early and convincing the business decision-maker that their organisation is the only one that can meet this need.

- Provide customer service at almost any cost – they are "always available".

- Sell in terms of benefits to the buying organisation and not in terms of product features.

- Try not to sell on price but on what the solution will do for the organisation – the price is small compared to the benefits you will get.

- Try to identify wants and care less about needs.

- Be driven by the need to achieve target/quota – whether monthly, quarterly or at year end – as this is how the bonus works.

- Be driven less by the need to make profit than by the need to sell volume and maximise the monetary value sold.

- Believe firmly in the power of human relationships – to the extent that they sometimes try to "sell" relationship.

- Concentrate on the relationship at the expense of the deal.

- Build rapport and gain trust, in order to persuade and get the sale – particularly with key business decision-makers.

- Try to get past the gatekeepers and go round the purchasing function, if possible to influence the business decision-makers.

- Like long-term deals and "partnerships" – these generate ongoing sales with little further effort.

- Happy to accept telephone orders, signed quotations etc. without formal purchase orders or contracts.

THE PROCUREMENT PROCESS

Procurement follows a well-defined process and is all about deciding what you are going to buy, how you are going to buy it, from whom you are going to buy it and on what commercial terms, and then going ahead to make the purchase. It does not stop there, however, as the goods/services/works need to be delivered and paid for, and the supplier must be managed to ensure that what was ordered is in fact delivered in the agreed way.

The procurement process is often referred to as the procurement lifecycle and can be drawn as follows:

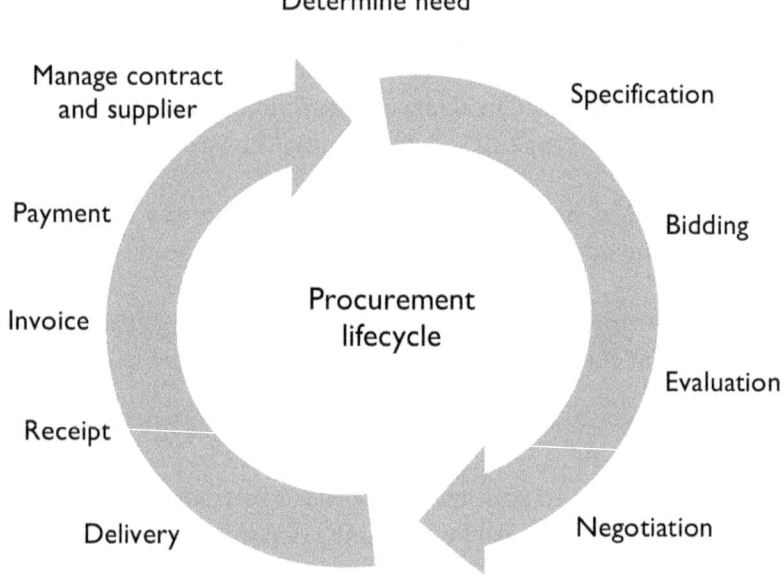

Diagram 5 – The procurement lifecycle

Most organisations have a purchasing function whose role it is to manage this process. The purchasing function is a support function that helps the business to buy things in the most effective way. In order to do this the function must be well aligned with the business; its managers and buyers must have excellent working relationships with their business colleagues.

The procurement process consists of the following steps:

Step 1: Determine the need

The business decides it needs to buy something. A good buyer will get involved at this stage to understand the need, help make sure that this is a need and not a "want", and to ensure that they keep in touch in the early stages where the business may already want to talk to potential suppliers. There is nothing wrong with this early involvement of suppliers, but the rules of engagement must be clear and commitment must be avoided.

Step 2: Write the specification

Once the need is fully understood, this is documented in the form of a written specification. It is normally the role of the business to write the specification but a good buyer will often assist by providing structure, ensuring clarity and deciding the level of detail. Where the need is clearly understood and tightly defined in technical terms, a detailed specification focusing on exactly what should be supplied will be written. On the other hand, where the need is less well defined and further input/options are required from suppliers, a more general specification focusing on what functions are required instead of exactly what should be supplied can be more appropriate.

Step 3: Get bids from suppliers

Bids are usually obtained from a number of suppliers, and the reliability of the bids obtained usually reflects the quality of the specification. A good buyer takes time to get to know the supply market well and to identify potential suppliers. These are often pre-qualified to ensure that they are financially sound, have the necessary experience and can meet quality criteria. A variety of bidding processes can be used, depending on circumstances. These include open tenders (anyone can bid), invitation tenders (of varying degrees of formality) where a number of pre-qualified suppliers are invited to bid, electronic auctions (where the specification is crystal clear and the only consideration is price), single-sourcing from one supplier (in areas of intense specialisation) and simply returning to the existing supplier (for political or relationship reasons).

In addition, objective bid-evaluation criteria are developed during this step, in order to prevent future bias.

Step 4: Evaluate bids

The bids are evaluated against the criteria developed at the bid stage, and a supplier is selected based on these. There is sometimes a split between technical and commercial evaluation, where the technical evaluation is carried out first. This has the advantage of trying to ensure that when commercial terms are compared, it is an apple-to-apple comparison.

Bid evaluation can involve tough internal discussions between the business and the buyer, where commercial advantage needs to be traded off against user preference or the difficulties involved in changing to a new supplier. Strategies vary, but in general a provisional choice is made at this stage and final negotiations are entered into with this supplier. Other potential suppliers are not informed until the negotiations have been successfully concluded and a contract signed.

Step 5: Negotiate contract

Final negotiations are entered into with the supplier, which (if all goes well) result in the signing of a contract. In simple cases a purchase order (or a signed quotation) will suffice, but a good buyer will always ensure that a minimum level of agreement is documented. This normally consists of definitions of specification, quality, volumes, price, payment terms and delivery.

There is always an internal approval process, and work should not start until approval is given and the contract is signed.

Step 6: Receive delivery, get invoice, pay

This is known as P2P (Purchase to Pay) and is often a very mechanical step. It is important, however, that it functions smoothly. Many organisations try to automate this step by use of purchasing software or the purchasing module of their financial system. Most systems start with a formal requisition (an internal statement of needs) followed by a formal purchase order (which can simply reference a signed contract). A delivery note is raised to confirm delivery and this is matched against the order. Then, when the invoice is received from the supplier, this is matched against the order too, and if all is well, payment is scheduled according to the agreed payment terms.

Step 7: Manage contract and manage supplier

Once the contract has been signed, it is followed up to ensure that the goods are delivered, the services are performed satisfactorily, or the works are carried out as agreed. Most purchasing functions categorise suppliers depending on how important they are to the organisation, and then dedicate management time to them accordingly. There are a few strategic suppliers (high value and/or high levels of collaboration) who are managed closely, and at the other extreme very many basic suppliers (lower value or one-off suppliers, or suppliers who can easily be substituted by others) to whom virtually no time is given.

THE SALES PROCESS

Just as procurement follows a well-defined process, so does sales. Sales is an area that has attracted huge amounts of management attention, and there is a vast industry propounding a variety of different approaches, all of which are claimed to lead to sales success. However, the basic process remains the same, and the differences arise mostly out of where the emphasis is placed in the process and on what exactly is being sold.

The process is all about identifying potential customers, following this up to establish a relationship, discovering the customer's needs and presenting a solution to meet these. Then objections to this solution are met, commitment is gained and the sale is closed.

As in procurement, where the process does not stop with the purchase, the sales process does not stop with the sale, but continues by following up to check on delivery, provide good customer service and build a relationship for the future.

The sales process can be drawn as follows:

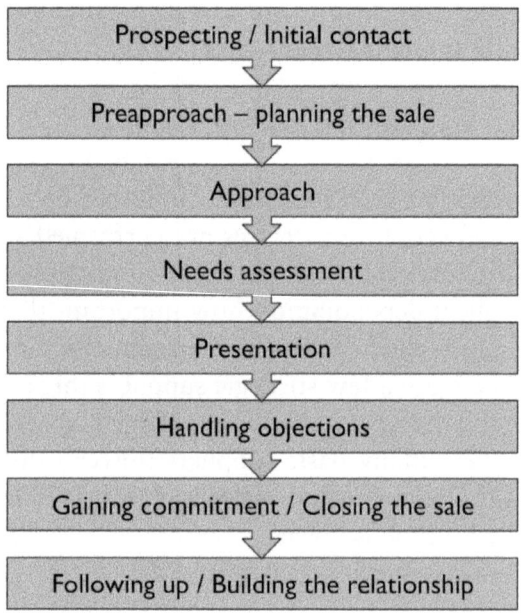

Diagram 6 – The sales process

Most organisations have a sales function whose role it is to manage this process. Unlike the purchasing function, the sales function is a key business function in its own right. In some organisations it is combined with marketing, depending on what is being sold; in others the sales process is managed by client directors or senior partners; and where a high degree of technical knowledge is required there is very close cooperation with technical functions.

The sales process consists of the following steps:

Step 1: Prospecting/Initial contact

Before planning a sale, a salesperson conducts research to identify the people or companies that might be interested in their product. At first, leads or potential buyers are identified; these are then followed up to identify prospects, where a prospect is a lead that is qualified to be ready, willing and able to buy. The point of qualifying leads is to allow the salesperson to concentrate on a) only those organisations which have identified a need and have the money to buy, and b) on the people within those organisations who have the authority to make a buying decision.

Step 2: Pre-approach – planning the sale

The pre-approach is where a good salesperson researches their prospects, familiarizing themselves with their potential customers' likely needs, and researching all the relevant background information they can about the individuals and their organisations.

Step 3: Approach

This is where the salesperson introduces themselves to their potential customers. This can take place in person, on the phone, via email or via some other online method. First impressions are judged to be very important, and time is invested in introductions, building rapport and then gaining trust.

Step 4: Needs assessment

Having made the approach, and having perhaps secured a meeting, the salesperson further investigates the potential customer's needs, trying to get behind opening statements to identify the "real" needs in some detail. In addition, time is taken to find out possible further areas for business in the short or long term and to discover who is likely to be involved in the decision-making process.

Step 4: Presentation

Once the needs are understood the salesperson makes a presentation or pitch. A good salesperson will by now have carried out a good deal of preparation and should understand their customer's needs well enough to be sure that a solution is offered which the customer could use. The pitch will be tailored to the potential customer, explaining how the product meets that person's or organisation's needs. The usual idea is to sell a solution, which meets the needs (involving of course the salesperson's product) rather than to sell the features of the product itself. Further ideas and possible options are often presented at this stage too.

Step 5: Handling objections

After the sales presentation has been made, the potential customer will have some hesitations or concerns, which are called objections. Good salespeople look at objections as opportunities to further understand and respond to customers' needs.

Step 6: Gaining commitment/Closing the sale

Eventually, if the potential customer is convinced that what is being offered will meet their needs, the sale is closed by agreeing on the terms and by signing a contract or writing a purchase order. Sometimes a salesperson has to make several trial closes, addressing further objections before the potential customer is ready to buy. It may turn out, even at this stage in the process, that the solution doesn't actually meet the needs, or that suitable commercial terms cannot be agreed or that the potential customer changes their mind, and so the sale falls through.

Step 7: Following up/Building the relationship

Following up involves staying in touch with the customer. First, by simply checking that the goods have been received in good condition, that services are being carried out well, or that the works have been performed to the customer's satisfaction. But the customer relationship has only just begun, and the aim of following up is to ensure customer satisfaction, retain customers, and get referrals and positive reviews.

Nowhere in the sales process is the word "negotiation" explicitly mentioned, although implicitly this is contained in the Presentation, Meeting Objections and Gaining Commitment steps. In anything but very simple situations it is unlikely that a serious sales negotiation on final terms and conditions would take place unless the "sale" itself had already been made.

APPENDIX 3

Partnerships, strategic and long-term relationships

INTRODUCTION

The word "partnership" is often rather inexactly used to describe longer-term or strategic relationships between buyers and sellers. This appendix explores these types of relationship further and covers:

- Types of relationship.

- Partnerships.

- The problem with long-term contracts.

- The advantages of long-term contracts.

- Management of long-term contracts.

TYPES OF RELATIONSHIP

In the extreme, relationships between buyer and seller can either be arm's length or collaborative:

- **Arm's length (or vertical):** This type of relationship usually exists where goods/services/works are simply bought and sold. The buyer takes possession and then uses the goods/services/ works for their own purposes without further cooperation from the supplier.

- **Collaborative (or horizontal):** This usually exists where the parties cooperate in a partnership or strategic alliance, and often involves a high degree of operational interaction between the parties over a longer period of time.

Arm's length relationships work well where there is clear agreement between buyer and seller on what is to be supplied and clear performance by the seller in accordance with the terms of this agreement

Collaborative relationships can be significantly harder to manage. The high level of operational interaction between the two parties can be difficult to control; they can create dependency (in either direction); disputes can develop about how value created should be distributed; and, the aims of each party can change over time. The collaboration can be buyer-dominated or supplier-dominated and it can be the case that the parties have different aims despite the fact that collaboration suits both parties at this point in time. When this is the case, one party can subsequently end the relationship to the disadvantage of the other; for example when a buyer has learnt vital skills from a supplier they could later decide to use these skills in house and dispense with the supplier.

In practice, things are never clear-cut, and relationships are often a mixture of arm's length and collaborative. There is often a history of previous trade between the parties and there can be personal links somewhere in the background. All this needs to be navigated with care.

PARTNERSHIPS

The word "partnership" can mean many things but is often used to promote a cooperative view of the world, where customers and suppliers form harmonious long-term relationships to mutual advantage. This is a world where "adversarial" negotiation is a thing of the past and where people work together to solve problems instead of apportioning blame. In practice, things do not often work out like this. If they did, then the marketplace would be lacking in the rough and tumble of competition that it needs to make it such a fascinating, innovative and productive place.

What is more likely to happen in practice is that organisations cooperate on one or more specific ventures (new product development, supply chain integration, information-sharing). Their overall objectives rightly remain intrinsically different, however, and this is a good reason for treating partnerships (in the sense of enduring long-term relationships) with utmost care. A wise prerequisite is the existence of a carefully negotiated agreement that sets out not only the terms and conditions of trade, but also the terms applying to the cooperation.

Buyers sometimes offer a long-term sole-supplier deal because it is the only way to get a lower price or to offload inventory. Sellers sometimes offer a long-term deal because it suits them to have guaranteed income. In neither case is there a hint of a real partnership.

The focus should normally be on what a relationship delivers and not on the relationship itself.

THE PROBLEM WITH LONG-TERM CONTRACTS

There are several basic issues with long-term contracts and care should be taken with any contract that ties the parties in for longer than one year. Such issues are:

- Things change over time and what works today does not necessarily work in three years' time.

- People change their minds, or new people come along, and they want to get out of the contract.

- They can create unhealthy dependency in both directions.

- They can take away exposure to the pressures of the market and can lead to stagnation.

- People forget that they need active management.

THE ADVANTAGES OF LONG-TERM CONTRACTS

Under certain circumstances long-term contracts can have advantages, but they should only be used with strategic suppliers and then only if there are compelling benefits. Such benefits could be:

- Significantly lower prices.

- Access to joint work on cost reduction.

- Integration of production and/or logistics leading to cost savings.

- Security of supply (in a market where there are few sources of supply).

- Access to innovation (which is especially for the buyer's organisation).

- In support of investment by the supplier (again especially for the buyer's organisation).

MANAGEMENT OF LONG-TERM CONTRACTS

Long-term contracts need appropriate management, and time and effort needs to be dedicated to this management if the benefits originally foreseen are to be realised in practice.

The contract itself will need special terms to regulate, for example: price variation; inflation; exchange-rate movements; raw-material price movements; ownership of jointly developed intellectual property etc. There also needs to be a clear definition of the circumstances under which termination is possible and just what the (financial) consequences of unplanned termination will be.

There needs to be a management structure in place to manage both the contract and the relationship with the other party. Roles and responsibilities need to be defined, and regular meetings with a fixed agenda should take place.

Appendix 4

Power in negotiation

Introduction

Power is the ability to achieve one's intended outcome when there is a conflict of interest between two parties. For example, a monopoly supplier has the power to increase price, and since there is no one else to buy from, this price rise is very hard to resist. In commercial negotiation, a seller will sometimes seek to increase their power by closing the market, using strategies such as owning patents, dominating the distribution channels or buying up the competition. A buyer will likewise seek to increase their power by using competitive pressure and opening up the market by encouraging or supporting new suppliers.

The word power can often have a bad connotation because many people associate the word with one party (unfairly) dominating or overpowering the other. In fact, power comes from many sources, can be real or apparent, and is closely connected to the ability to influence people or situations. Power is intrinsically neither good nor bad, but it is the abuse of power that gives cause for concern.

The following points are worth considering:

- **Sources of power:** how can power arise, and in what form?

- **Rules of power:** power has some rules of its own, which govern how it affects people and situations.

- **Abuse of power:** power can be used wisely, or it can be abused.

- **Perceptions of power:** it is your perceptions about who has the power that really count.

- **Measuring power:** at least one writer on negotiation has set out a method of more objectively measuring power.

These will be considered in turn.

SOURCES OF POWER

It is useful to consider what can give power to a party in a negotiation and possible sources of power are listed below:

- **Positional power (power of legitimate authority):** this is the natural power that comes with positions of (legitimate) authority or is gained by reputation.

- **Rewards:** the power that comes from offering incentives or bonuses, and in the extreme case through the giving and taking of bribes.

- **Sanctions (the opposite of rewards):** the ability of a supplier to withdraw supply, or of a buyer to exclude a seller from the bidder's list, are expressions of their power.

- **Physical force:** this is rare in commercial negotiations.

- **Expertise:** this is common in the hi-tech world or where dealing with scarce skills.

- **Information:** if you know more about something than the other party, then you have power. This is known as "information asymmetry" in negotiation-speak or more colloquially by the phrase, "information is power".

- **Commitment:** where one party is prepared to go to great lengths to get something done (far more than the other party), this leads to an increase in power for this party.

- **Charisma:** this is the power of personality to charm, or in extreme cases to deceive.

- **Having an alternative:** because you have an alternative you do not have to continue to negotiate and accept less favourable terms.

- **Time:** a lack of time can lead to a loss of power.

- **Monopoly:** a limited source of supply gives power to the seller; competitors give power to the buyer.

- **Relationship:** the negative power of a bad relationship can be damaging.

RULES OF POWER

A number of aspects and qualities of power in negotiations have been identified, and these are listed below. Sometimes these are known as the "rules of power":

- **Seldom does one party have all the power.**

- **Power is relative between the parties:** there is no absolute definition of power, and it can only be said that one party has more or less power than the other, or that the power of each party lies in different areas.

- **Power is limited:** even though a supplier has the power to deny you supply, this power is limited by considerations of when this might be used responsibly or what it might do to the relationship.

- **You have more power than you may at first realise:** it is worth spending time to carefully consider possible sources of power and to take practical steps to increase your power. For a start, there is the temptation to dwell on your weaknesses, whereas the other party will show their strengths and keep their weaknesses hidden.

- **Power may be real or apparent:** it is in one party's interest to make the other party think that they have less power than they have, as in this case they might be more likely to concede to requests or in the extreme to demands or threats.

- **Power exists only as far as it is accepted:** the use of power by one party is only effective to the extent that the other party responds with the desired behaviour. For example, a supplier might raise prices without discussion, but if the buyer then simply buys from elsewhere, then the exercise of this power has had no effect. You always have three choices when someone tries to exercise power over you – yes, no, or trade.

- **The exercise of power has advantages and disadvantages.**

- **The balance of power in relationships can (and usually does) change over time.**

- **Negotiating power is increased by the ability to endure uncertainty:** if a party is not afraid to break off negotiations (and thus increase uncertainty), to explore whether a better deal is available elsewhere, then this increases their power.

- **The side with the fewer constraints (or more alternatives) generally holds the most power:** if the seller has to make the sale by a certain date to hit the year-end target but the buyer has no such constraint, then the buyer has more power.

ABUSE OF POWER

Just because you can do something, it doesn't always mean that you should. The holding of power comes with the need to exercise it responsibly. For example, a buyer might hold the power to take business away from a long-term supply-partner and give it to someone else. It pays to think carefully before this sort of step is taken and any such decision should ideally be supported by the following considerations:

- Is this a reasonable step in the circumstances, or are there other alternatives?

- Who is the supplier (large or small)? Is the supplier heavily dependent on the buying organisation? What effect will the termination of business have on the supplier?

- How great is the gain for the buying organisation?

- Does the relationship matter – in the short and long term?

- Where this action is being taken as a sanction for poor performance, does the punishment match the crime?

PERCEPTIONS OF POWER

In practice, your perception of your power is what really counts as this will influence how you behave. If you believe that you have power over the other party, then you are likely to be more optimistic about the outcome of the negotiation; the more powerful you feel that the other party is, the less well you expect to do. Perceptions of power are subject to all kinds of influence and it has been shown that very often these are based on the flimsiest of data.

Experienced aggressive negotiators can take advantage of this lack of evidence, using streetwise manipulation to make you believe that they have more power than they have or that you have less, and therefore you should concede to their wishes.

A simple ploy based on this is to assert that something is non-negotiable – "my hands are tied…" For example a buyer could say that payment terms are 90 days because that is company policy set by the (faceless) finance function located a long way away in the organisation's headquarters. Whether these are truly non-negotiable depends on the power balance and whether the organisation really has the power to force these terms upon you.

The point of the assertion is to manipulate you to concur without thinking about it, because you believe it to be true. Some organisations do have rigid payment terms that are never conceded, but have you checked the facts to see if this is one of them?

Such assertions should at the very least be tested or challenged, and possible responses include in this case, "that's a shame, our standard is 30 days; this is a point we will need to discuss later," or, "if you would accept a price rise of 5%, we would be prepared to consider increased payment terms."

It pays to think very carefully in advance about your sources of power and those of the other party, and to try to come up with a reasonable assessment in advance, based on facts; this assessment should be continually reviewed during the negotiation itself. If faced with dubious assertions of power, you should pause and think about what is going on, and if necessary take a break to check the facts and reassess your perceptions of where the power lies.

MEASURING POWER

When assessing how much power you have, it helps if you can do this objectively. Atkinson, in chapter 8 of his book *Negotiate the Best Deal* (Director Books, 1990), sets out what he calls "a practical way of defining and using power" as a means of objective assessment. The method makes a systematic analysis of the situation but still depends on making assumptions about some factors of influence. Even if these assumptions prove to be inaccurate, however, the very act of making such an analysis and considering these factors is beneficial.

APPENDIX 5

Tradables

INTRODUCTION

Tradables are simply what we have available to trade. They have a value, but this depends on who is making the valuation and is usually different for each party. When trading, you should aim to achieve your target value for an item, and this is often expressed as a range of possible values from your most desirable to your least desirable. Your opening position (the seller's opening bid for example) expresses your Most Desirable Outcome (MDO) and the point at which you exercise your BATNA (your Best Alternative to a Negotiated Agreement) expresses your Least Desirable Outcome (LDO). Somewhere in between lies your real interest, what you would ideally like to achieve.

This appendix covers the following points:

- Tradables.

- Cost, price and value.

- Positions and interests.

- MDOs, LDOs and the ZoMA.

- A list of potential tradables.

TRADABLES

We trade because we value things differently; if we didn't value things differently we would not have disagreements and there would be no need for negotiations!

Tradables represent possible points for discussion and agreement, and it is useful to generate as many as possible. By having a number of tradables available to discuss, you increase the chances of finding some common ground around which agreement can be reached.

For example, if the negotiation is focused solely on price then it may degenerate into deadlock where no agreement on a price acceptable to both parties is possible. However, if the option exists to talk about trading payment terms, volumes, contract start date, length of contract etc., then it might be possible to link price to one or more of these and so find an agreement. Sometimes this is known as "expanding the pie" and it gets away from viewing negotiation as a means of distributing a fixed amount of resource. You can generate a surprising number of options by brainstorming, sometimes together with the other party. But you should not fall into the trap of moving from negotiating to joint problem solving. It is your job, in an arm's length transaction to buy or sell goods/services/works, to negotiate the best deal for your party and not a deal, for example, that delivers a "fair profit" for the seller or a "fair price" for the buyer, whatever those terms mean.

We briefly considered tradables earlier, in chapter 1, and again in chapter 3, and noted that we often trade things that have a different value to us than they do to the other party. Thus you should be very clear about not only what you consider to be your tradables but also what value you attach to them. You should also make reasoned assumptions about what value the other party might attach to the same tradable and whether the other party would consider the same things to be tradables.

In considering these issues, it can be very helpful to think about non-negotiables, and then proceed on the basis that everything else is negotiable or tradable! However, it is also wise to challenge just why you consider a non-negotiable to be a non-negotiable – is there a good reason?

COST, PRICE AND VALUE

The issue of value is worth thinking about clearly, because you need to know the value of a tradable in order to trade it successfully.

Price is to some extent set by cost, but to a much greater extent by the market in which the item is to be bought or sold. The "law" of supply and demand determines the price. The market of course can be very imperfect. For example, large monopoly suppliers have the power to manipulate price and regulators have the power to intervene in this case. In some cases, politics influences price by setting the level of import tariffs or agricultural subsidies.

Cost can help to set a minimum price at which you are prepared to sell something, and indeed if overall you do not sell things for more than they have cost you to supply, then (unless you are subsidised from elsewhere) your organisation will go out of business. However, this says nothing about how you may wish to price an individual transaction, as you might be prepared to sell something below its cost in order to gain something of more value to you (such as a reduction in considerable amounts of stock). Cost can be hard to calculate too. As a minimum, cost will have components of direct cost and overheads, and there is always the question of how overheads should be allocated. When something has taken time and effort to develop, such as software, then there is also the question of how these development costs should be allocated.

Value is neither cost nor price, although you should consider these when trying to assess value. Value takes into account other qualities, including:

• **Social:** for example, transport in rural areas provides a valuable service, but hardly ever covers its costs; it is subsidised from elsewhere.

- **Branding:** branding is there just for that, to create value in one form or another. The McKinsey brand is strong in management consultancy, for example, and McKinsey consultants command a high price.

- **Quality:** high quality goods last longer than lower quality goods and suffer from fewer breakdowns.

- **Innovation:** if you can provide innovation specific to your customer's needs, this has value.

- **Technology:** if you have technology that few other organisations have, this has value. You could licence this technology, for example.

- **Risk:** if you can reduce risk by supplying a more reliable product, this has value.

- **Industry trends:** if you can spot industry trends and be one of the first organisations to be in a new market, for example, this has value.

- **Competitive advantage:** anything you can do that your competitors can't, has value.

- **Creative talent:** if you have truly great talent then this has value. In the marketing world, creative talent is highly valued.

- **Sentimental:** some items have little value in terms of market price, but have a meaning to their owner which confers real value.

Value can be hard to measure and you should first identify the value of a tradable in qualitative terms before trying to put a monetary value to it. From a buyer's point of view, selling value will only work if you can quantify that value in terms of money or, failing that, making it very clear in graphic terms just what that value is.

Calculating the total cost of ownership (TCO) is one way of looking beyond raw price. It is a technique that estimates how much ownership of the goods/services/works will cost you over their lifetime. It is more usually done by buyers when they wish to compare bids with different features. Drinkalot could do this in this case, by assuming a ten-year life for the accounting system, taking the purchase price and then adding to it estimates for replacement costs, consumables costs, maintenance fees etc. over this period.

However, TCO would not allow Drinkalot to calculate the value to be gained from good use of the business analysis software. Here, an estimate of additional sales is necessary, which of course is not at all easy to come by. You should also remember that what is really of interest here is the additional value that Computalot would provide by selling consultancy related to the use of this software, compared to the value Drinkalot would get if there were no consultancy or if the consultancy were performed by a different organisation with less experience. This is perhaps easier to calculate, as you could argue that this boils down to a matter of time. Buying consultancy from Computalot, for example, could mean that Drinkalot were able to get an estimated 0.5% extra sales for a period of three months. After that, Drinkalot would have figured out how to use the software themselves.

Thinking about value can also help generate more tradables. You can make a list of your sources of value, knowing that each one of these is also a tradable, even if you don't necessarily want to trade it.

POSITIONS AND INTERESTS

It is useful to consider exactly what is under discussion during a negotiation. What is spoken about is often a position, but behind this position lie issues and interests, as follows:

- **Positions:** a position is what is actually expressed during the discussion as a need or want. For example, the Computalot says, "the price of these computers is £100,000".

- **Issues:** the issue is what we are talking about. In this case, the price of the computers themselves. If Drinkalot says "I will offer you £60,000 for the computers" they are taking a different position on the issue of price. An issue is not necessarily a tradable. For example, if you are talking about the issue of who owns IP (Intellectual Property) but for you this is non-negotiable (you have to own the IP) then this issue is not a tradable.

- **Interests:** behind issues and positions often lie interests. An interest gives us the answer to why a party is talking about this or that issue and taking this or that position on it. In this case, Computalot's interest could be to maximise the profit from the sale or they could be simply want to make a sale at a reasonable profit in order to meet the half-yearly sales target. Drinkalot's interest could be to restrict the seller's profit to the industry average, or to make certain savings that are needed to hit the annual savings target.

Knowing the interests that lie behind positions can help to identify all the issues at stake and widen the scope of discussion. This can lead to the discovery of alternatives, move the negotiation from value claiming to value creating, and allow the pie to be expanded. Knowing that a seller is interested in meeting their sales target, for example, could allow them to accept a reduced price in return for a quick sale or increased volumes, or both.

Negotiation based on an understanding of your own and the other party's interests is preferred to a negotiation based solely on positions. Your interests represent your needs, hopes and concerns, and there may be several ways of meeting these. Whereas your positions are pre-defined statements about how exactly you want these needs to be met. The problem with positions is that you can get attached to them and forget what you really need to achieve.

One way around this is to bear in mind that all prices are fictitious, in the sense that they do not necessarily represent the price at which you will buy or sell, or the conditions that may be attached to that price. When a price is first named it should be simply viewed for what it is – a position – a way of starting a discussion about the issue of price. Behind this position may lie all sorts of considerations about volumes, payment terms and date of purchase. If the negotiation simply focuses on price, these further considerations and the real interests of the parties may well get lost.

MDOs, LDOs and the ZoMA

It was discussed earlier that there is no right answer in negotiation, and this can be illustrated in the following diagram, which considers only the issue of price:

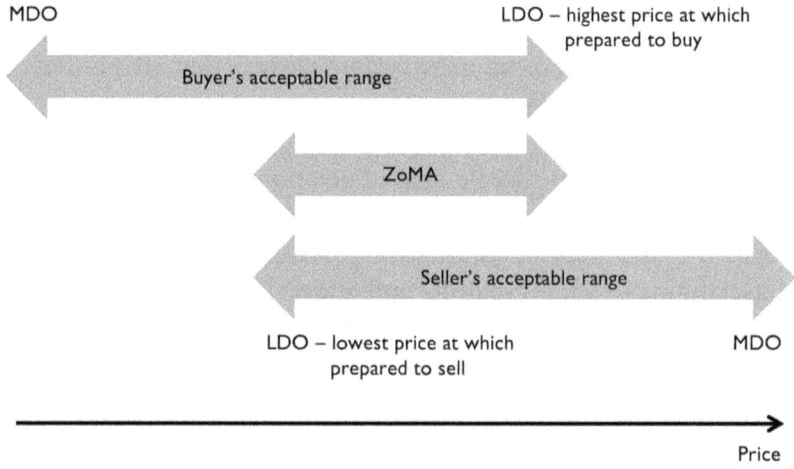

Diagram 7 – MDOs, LDOs and the ZoMA

Both the buyer and seller have an LDO (Least Desirable Outcome) and an MDO (Most Desirable Outcome). Somewhere in between these two extremes lies a price that satisfies their interests.

For the buyer, the LDO is the highest price they are prepared to pay and this is the price that they are prepared to use their BATNA (buy from another organisation, who offers a lower price). The MDO is the lowest price they are prepared to pay, which in theory perhaps has no limits, but practical considerations usually restrict this to the lowest credible price in the market.

From the seller's point of view, their MDO is their opening position, as revealed in their bid. Their LDO is the price at which they are prepared to use their BATNA (and seek another buyer).

You can see from the diagram that there is a range of possible prices that would theoretically satisfy both parties and this is known as the ZoMA (Zone of Mutual Agreement). There is no right price, and the negotiation is driven by the desire of each party to agree a price as close to their MDO as possible. The MDO and LDO of the other party are of course not known at the start of the negotiation, although you should make some reasonable assumptions as part of your preparation.

It is possible of course that the price expectations due not overlap and there is no ZoMA. In which case, if price is the only issue under consideration, then, unless one party revises their expectations, the use of negotiation will not reach an agreement on price. However, as soon as you add other tradables (and again, each will have its LDOs, MDOs and ZoMA), we regain the possibility of reaching an agreement. A reduction in price could be traded for a reduction in payment terms – you get your money more quickly – for example.

ALTERNATIVES AND BATNA

If a negotiation seems to be heading in the wrong direction and an agreement on terms that you could accept seems unlikely, then you need to know your alternative; your Plan B.

It is best to consider alternatives carefully in advance because it is easy to lose sight of them made in the heat of the negotiation event. It is easy to continue to negotiate when in fact there is a better alternative.

This better alternative is often known as a BATNA (Best Alternative to a Negotiated Agreement) and you may have a number of BATNAs covering different issues under negotiation.

A LIST OF POTENTIAL TRADABLES

As covered earlier, it pays to think hard about what you are willing to trade and what you are not willing to trade. Although each negotiation is different, a list is provided below of terms which often need to be considered when reaching agreement on commercial contracts. By considering each term and deciding how this is relevant in your case, you can construct a list of tradables, together with your position(s) and interest(s), similar to that laid out in chapter 3.

Basic commercial terms:

- **Specification:** what exactly are the goods/services/works to be supplied?

- **Quality/Standards of performance:** to what quality standards should goods be supplied or services/works be performed?

- **Volumes:** how much will be delivered during the length of the contract? Is there a commitment to buy a certain volume?

- **Price:** how much will the buyer pay to acquire the goods/services/works?

- **Payment terms:** when does the price have to be paid, and how long has the buyer to pay once an invoice is received?

- **Delivery and timings:** where, when and how are the goods/services/works to be delivered? When does the contract start and how long will it last?

Other commercial terms, where the relationship is more strategic:

- **Access to innovation:** a supplier may have some interesting innovations which the buyer wants access to on an exclusive or semi-exclusive basis.

- **New product development:** the buyer and seller cooperate to bring new (innovative) products to the market.

- **Supplier performance improvement:** the supplier is targeted to improve their performance in a number of areas such as quality, delivery times, maintenance costs etc.

- **Joint cost reduction:** the parties jointly work to reduce costs, by for example redesigning parts or processes.

- **Supply chain optimisation:** the parties work together to manage stock, deliveries etc. as efficiently as possible.

Other points for agreement:

- **Term and termination:** how long does the contract last and under what circumstances can either party terminate the contract?

- **Price variation:** how is price regulated in long-term contracts? Is it linked to inflation? Must it be renegotiated each year, and what happens if there is no agreement?

- **Confidentiality and data protection:** what needs to be kept confidential by whom?

- **Intellectual property (IP) rights:** who owns any IP created by the contract?

- **Law and jurisdiction:** which country's law governs the contract and which courts are responsible for its interpretation?

- **Title:** when does title to goods, or ownership of works, pass to the buyer?

- **Point of delivery, risk, duty and insurance:** in international trade this is often regulated by reference to INCOTERMS. Which of these will apply?

- **Letters of credit, guarantees and bonds:** what third-party provisions (such as Bank Guarantees, Performance Bonds, Letters of Credit) are made to ensure delivery from the supplier or payment from the buyer.

- **Warranty:** what warranties are made about the goods/services/works and for how long?

- **Force majeure:** under what conditions out of the parties' control can the contract be suspended or ended?

- **Liability, indemnity and consequential loss:** what happens if the supplier causes damage or if use of his goods/services causes damage to third parties? Are damages linked to direct loss only or is consequential loss (for example, loss of business) included?

- **Penalties, incentives and liquidated damages:** will the supplier be penalised for late delivery or incentivised to deliver early?

- **Insurance:** what sort of insurance must the supplier carry and to what amount?

APPENDIX 6

A communicator's toolkit

INTRODUCTION

Good, clear, effective communication is vital to success in negotiation. Communication is a subject in its own right and a good source of information is Ros Howard and Steve Mallaband's *Building Excellence in Business Communication* (Grosvenor House Publishing, planned early 2015).

In general, a skilled communicator will know how to:

- Define the purpose of their communication.

- Understand their audience.

- Define and structure their message.

- Choose the best method of delivery.

- Listen.

- Ask pertinent questions and give well thought-out answers.

- Summarise.

- Lead discussions.

Based on these skills, a communicator's toolkit can be assembled as follows:

PURPOSE

It is important that the purpose of your communication is clear to yourself before you begin to communicate to others. Most communication can be allocated to one of eight generic purpose categories as follows:

- Inform and give advice.

- Persuade, influence or convince a person or group of people to change.

- Sell something or a new idea.

- Help understanding.

- Stimulate discussion/be controversial.

- Entertain.

- Share an interest.

- Motivate.

By considering these categories, you can decide which one your message falls into, and then add the subject you need to cover. For example:

- "To **inform** the other party of your opening bid."

- "To **persuade** the other party to consider your need for a price rise."

- "To **stimulate discussion** on the different options available for trading during the negotiation."

- "To **motivate** the other party to make some constructive proposals during the negotiation."

Any of these highlighted words would make a good working title for your message, and will help to keep you on track.

Understanding your audience

You need to know and understand the audience with whom you are communicating, so that you can communicate in terms that they will understand and buy into. The more you know about your audience the better, and in terms of a negotiation you should try and find out the following about the other party:

- **Number:** how many people will there be at the negotiation event, and what are their names?

- **Role:** what is their role in their organisation; what is their role in the negotiation?

- **Influence:** what is the limit of their influence within their organisation?

- **Knowledge:** how much do they know about the subject of the negotiation? How much will you have to explain and how much knowledge can you assume?

- **Language:** will the negotiation be conducted in their native tongue? How much care should you take to avoid long and complicated explanations?

Defining and structuring your message

It is important not only to decide just what you want to communicate, but also to structure your message, so that your audience understands it easily. When thinking of what you wish to communicate, think also of what you do not wish to communicate. In a negotiation you do not want the other party to find out too quickly just what your LDOs (Least Desirable Outcomes) and your BATNAs (Best Alternatives to a Negotiated

Agreement) are. When structuring your message, think about keeping it short and simple, so that it is readily understood. Do not try to put too much information into one message – three key points at most is a working rule

When composing and structuring a longer communication, such as a written bid, ensure that it is broken down into logical sections and is prefaced by a summary.

Remember that you know more about your message than your audience; otherwise they wouldn't need to listen to you. So you may need to use repetition and give your audience time to take things in.

DELIVERY

Once you have clearly structured your message, you can choose the best method of delivering it. This could be via post, fax, a telephone call, an email, a formal presentation, a legal document, a teleconference, a videoconference, or face to face during a meeting or a negotiation event etc. You should think about both what format will best serve your purpose and what help that format can give your audience.

In the case of negotiations, the opening bid could be sent by email, fax or post, for example, and could be followed up by a formal presentation with questions and answers. Telephone calls will be necessary to clarify points prior to the negotiation event and these can also be an opportunity to try to condition the expectations of the other party. The negotiation event normally takes place face to face, but where the parties are geographically spread a videoconference might be used. A legal or quasi-legal document might be appropriate for documenting the agreement reached at the end of the negotiation.

You should be prepared to present your information in a variety of ways, as different people grasp things differently. For example, some people find graphs difficult to interpret, others have difficulty with spreadsheets and others love both. If you find yourself getting frustrated at someone's apparent inability to grasp your point, you should consider presenting it in a different manner.

There are a variety of tools that can be used to help your audience understand your message, depending on how it is delivered, including:

- **Verbal:** speak clearly and at the right pace; give your audience time to take in the message.

- **Non-verbal:** in face-to-face communication (and to a lesser extent in telephone or video communication), be aware of non-verbal communication such as tone of voice and body-language and make sure your body-language matches what you say. This is dealt with separately in appendix 7.

- **Words:** use as few words as possible to make the point; use reasonably simple language and short sentences; avoid using too many idioms or clichés. If your audience includes non-native speakers this is even more important. Remember that business communication is not there to win literary prizes.

- **Illustrations:** words on their own can be very dry, and to reinforce a point use cartoons, photographs, flowcharts, graphs, tables, spreadsheets etc. However, make sure these are carefully chosen, do actually make the point and are not there just as decoration.

- **Visual aids:** use visual aids such as flipcharts, whiteboards and PowerPoint presentations. Mind maps can be useful when brainstorming; hand-outs can also be useful in support of presentations, particularly for those not working in their native language, where a pre-meeting hand-out gives more time for understanding; templates can be used to structure how you wish to see information presented.

- **Story-telling:** stories, anecdotes, metaphors and allegories can be useful to make a point, but you should use them with care. A story is but a story (not a universal truth), anecdotes are often exaggerated and what looks like a nice metaphor to you can leave your audience wondering what you are talking about.

- **Tactile:** this can include the use of models, mock-ups, product samples and plant visits. These are perhaps more appropriate for the pre-negotiation stage of buying and selling, but remember that the setting for a negotiation event can communicate a "feel" about you and your organisation, or about the party you are dealing with, depending on whether you are the host or not.

LISTENING

Listening in silence is a powerful tool, and here are some pointers to help you do this well:

- **Listen actively:** don't just wait for others to finish speaking to get your counter-point in, but use empathy while the other person is talking, and try to fully understand their point of view.

- **Show you are listening:** simple nodding can be effective.

- **Watch your body-language:** relax, as being stiff and rigid in posture can send the wrong message to the other party – that you are not being open-minded and not really giving them your attention.

- **If a question occurs to you:** jot it down and ask at it the end.

- **It is fine to take notes:** but do not scribble and write while looking down the entire time another person is speaking.

- **Do not be distracted:** have your phone and your emails switched off, for example.

ASKING QUESTIONS AND GIVING ANSWERS

Don't be afraid to ask questions, and keep going until you understand the answers and get the information you need. Kipling's six honest serving men (what, why when, how, where, who), whom we met in chapter 3 of the book, are a good guide to the sort of question to ask.

Questions can be categorised into two fundamentally different types – open and closed, although in practice some questions have aspects of both:

- **Open questions:** These are generally used to elicit an explanation or even just to keep the discussion going. For example, "can you explain how you arrived at this figure?" or, "what do you think the market is doing at the moment?"

- **Closed questions:** These are used to elicit precise information or to check facts, and require a definite response, such as "yes" or "no". For example, "can your finance function process an invoice in less than ten days?" or, "are you saying that we have made over ten late deliveries in the last two weeks?"

Both types of question have their place in negotiation and a judicious mixture of both, depending on where the discussions are heading is likely to be the best tactic. Open questions have the disadvantage that vague answers can nearly always be given, and closed questions such as, "is that your best offer?" are at best a waste of time (a supplier is unlikely to say "no" to this question) and at worst can obstruct further discussion.

Questions can be used for several reasons:

- **Opening up the discussion:** here, open questions are used to get the discussion going or keep it going. "What do you think about our latest additions to the product range?"

- **Eliciting information, the facts:** here the emphasis is on getting information, or the facts about the matter. "Have you had any thoughts about what you could bring to us in terms of innovation?"

- **Clarifying information:** here the emphasis is on clarifying what has been given in answer to a previous question. If the answer to the above question were, "yes we've had two or three ideas actually," then to clarify this and add precision, the next question might be, "can you tell us more about each one please?"

- **Building on what has been said:** here questions and answers can be a useful way of capturing and developing ideas. If one of the innovations referred to above concerned enhancing the organisation's image, then the questions and answers could conceivably develop as follows into a mini brainstorming session:

"We thought we might be able to use highly-targeted PR to reach specific age-groups,"

"Which age-groups have you got in mind and how would you reach them?"

"We'd need to work on that together in detail, but maybe twenty- to thirty-year-olds who use special-interest websites. What do you think...?"

- **Closing down the discussion:** closed questions can be used to check agreement at the end of a discussion and allow things to move on in another direction. "So, we can agree on that point, can we?"

- **Manipulate the other party:** trick questions can also be used to manipulate the other party. For example:

"We're both in agreement here, aren't we" is a **leading question** because it invites the answer "yes".

"Don't you trust me?" is a **loaded question** because to answer either "yes" (when you don't actually trust them) or "no" (which, even if you don't trust them, can be hard to say) is the wrong answer.

You can deal with such tricks by being honest and finding a nice way to be so. A positive answer to the first question above could be, "well, we're getting there slowly," and a good way of replying to the second is, "it's not a matter of trust here; my experience tells me that however genuine you personally are in your commitment to pay us on time, it's usually down to the finance function to determine what happens in practice."

- **Check intent:** ask yourself if what you are doing is in the best interests of your organisation.

When answering questions, it may well be that you do not in fact want to answer the question, or at least not yet. For example, the question, "what is the highest price you will pay for these goods?" put early in a negotiation should not get a direct answer. In fact, you have several choices:

- **Answer with a question:** "Well, why don't you tell me what the lowest price is that you have sold them for this year?"

- **Question the question:** "Why are you asking me that? It depends on so many things and that's what we're here to discuss today!"

- **Duck the question:** "You surely can't expect me to answer that!"

- **Defer the question:** "Let's talk about that later, once we've covered the rest of the points on the list."

Lying is not a good idea. Lies usually destroy trust and ultimately relationships. It is also not a good idea to withhold information if you do not have a good reason to do so, as sharing information can be a good way of solving problems, particularly if you have a high degree of trust with the other party.

SUMMARISING

Playing back a summary of what has been discussed is an excellent means of checking that understanding has been reached. The language of summaries includes the use of such phrases as: "What it sounds like you are saying is...." "Am I correct in thinking that...?" "Let's just check we all agree on the following points...."

Summaries can be used to:

- **Check for understanding:** communication between humans can be difficult and imprecise. Use summaries at regular intervals to check that your messages have been understood and that you have understood the messages from the other party.

- **Check assumptions:** by listening to answers to your questions and by observing what questions the other party asks, you will not only gain factual information, but you will also start to make assumptions about what has perhaps not been said. Assumptions can be dangerous, in that they can be wrong. Making a summary which includes your assumptions and inviting comment is a good way of checking these and learning more.

- **Invite challenge:** a summary can be put up to invite challenge and thus stimulate discussion. You can also use this to check assumptions by including an assumption in the summary. If it doesn't get challenged then you were correct; if it gets challenged, however, then, although you may not find out all you want, you will almost certainly learn more about your assumption.

LEADING DISCUSSIONS

You should remain in control of discussions, making sure that they remain constructive and do not descend into arguments or recriminations. You should consider the following points:

- **Participation:** remember that for some people simply being a part of the process is equally important as the issues under discussion. In individualistic cultures everyone wants to be heard, but in more collective or hierarchical cultures people may need to be encouraged to speak.

- **Opinions:** an opinion is just an opinion – a view held by someone. It is not the truth and you are under no obligation to agree with it. However, this does not mean that people should be prevented from expressing their opinions or that their opinions should not be accorded respect.

- **Positive language:** use positive language and be encouraging. This keeps the discussion going, helps to improve understanding between the parties and builds trust. Be direct and use I/We to convey thoughts, feelings and opinions, rather than dealing in the abstract.

- **Negative language:** avoid this so far as possible, and use the word "no" sparingly. Interruption, blaming, scoring points, making threats etc. should be avoided.

  "We feel frustrated when you fail to deliver on time because we then have to slow down our production and pay staff to stay later," works much better than saying, "you are lazy and never meet deadlines."

- **Use a variety of techniques:** questions to gather information, answers to impart information, silence when there is nothing to be said, summaries to check for understanding etc.

- **Speak on your own behalf:** do not speak on behalf of others; this is not only dangerous in that it is based on an assumption about what the other person wants to say, but is also highly demotivating. Encourage people to speak for themselves.

APPENDIX 7

Non-verbal communication
and body language

INTRODUCTION

Non-verbal communication can take many forms and John Adair lists the following nine in his book *Effective Communication: The Most Important Management Skill of All* (Pan 2009):

- Facial expression.
- Eye contact.
- Tone of voice.
- Physical touch.
- Appearance (clothes, hair).
- Body/posture.
- Proximity.
- Physical gestures (hand and foot movements).
- Head position.

These are often grouped under the single title of "body language".

BODY LANGUAGE

Body language is a whole subject in its own right and a useful source of information is James Borg's *Body Language: How to Know What's Really Being Said* (Pearson, 2013). A great deal of caution is needed here however; extravagant claims about the power of body language are made, some of what is presented is dressed-up common sense and there are many myths concerning its use. Some of these are nicely explored by Dr. Alex Drewnicky in *Body Language: Common Myths and How to Use it Effectively* (web, 2013).

Humans by nature can "read" body language, but as in all things some do this better than others. Equally, some humans are better at concealing the bodily expression of their thoughts and feelings than others. In negotiation you should certainly look for non-verbal communication, but should treat what you learn as assumptions and find ways of testing these. Similarly you should be wary of giving away non-verbally what you do not wish the other party to know.

Points to consider are:

- **The 55-38-7 rule:** based on work done by Albert Mehrabian at the University of Los Angeles in 1971, it is widely quoted that 55% of communication between humans is based on visual body language, 38% is based on vocal language (how we say things, not what we say) and only 7% is based on what we say.

    This is often misinterpreted to mean that the words are not important, whereas they are in fact vitally important. What the research actually showed was that the words are far more likely to be believed if they are backed up by a matching tone of voice and reinforced by appropriate body language. Whereas the words carry the information in the message, the visual and vocal body language carry the attitudes, thoughts and feelings.

- **Mismatching:** Where the 55-38-7 statistic is really powerful is if the verbal and non-verbal parts of the communication do not match. In this case, you should take care to find out what the message really is: should you rely on the verbal part (the non-verbal mismatch signifying nervousness or poor delivery, for example), or does the non-verbal content signify that what is being said lacks personal conviction or contains distortions of the truth? Equally, a message delivered where the verbal and non-verbal content are well aligned can be a very powerful message.

- **Trust:** if we do not like someone or do not trust someone then it also pays to pay more attention to the non-verbal content of the message.

- **Masking:** humans are often good at masking their thoughts and feelings, and learn how to present a happy confident exterior, for example, when they feel far from happy and confident inside. Effective negotiators can be particularly good at this and thus their body language may not be a reliable source of information at all.

- **Myths:** it is almost certainly a myth that you can tell when a person is lying through the observation of their body language. It is also untrue that crossed arms always signal a "no"; the person could simply be cold or feel more comfortable that way.

- **Assumptions:** it is certainly useful to observe body language, and an understanding of how it might be interpreted is a useful communication skill. However, any interpretation of what you observe should be treated as an assumption and tested in practice during the negotiation event.

APPENDIX 8

Measuring personality

INTRODUCTION

Personality is hard to define, but can be understood by considering that you display a number of personality traits that predispose you to behave in certain ways. These traits mark you personally and as a whole make up your personality.

There are many psychological tests that have been designed to measure personality. For example:

- Myers Briggs Type Indicator (MBTI).

- Sixteen Personality Factor Questionnaire (16PF).

- Minnesota Multiphasic Personality Inventory (MMPI).

Some are general and others measure specific traits. Psychologists would normally use a number of these tests in order to assess someone's personality.

If you are interested in exploring a way of looking at personality and its effect on negotiating behaviour, then you should use an appropriate tool. One possibility here is the Thomas-Kilmann Conflict Style Instrument (TKI), which uses a model that looks at five different dimensions of personality.

EFFECT OF PERSONALITY ON NEGOTIATING BEHAVIOUR

Understanding personality certainly has its role in negotiation, but it also has its limitations. Its biggest use would be if you could accurately predict someone's behaviour from knowing his or her personality. This is not easy for a trained psychologist let alone for a commercial negotiator, and a little knowledge here can be a dangerous thing. It is always better to observe behaviour and respond appropriately.

You should consider the following:

- **Personality is not necessarily stable:** people often have multiple mini-personalities, which they use for different situations.

- **Masking:** people can be good at masking certain personality traits, donning a negotiation persona and managing their behaviour. The masking sometimes falls away to reveal a different personality, when someone is under stress.

- **Remain in control:** when you are in control, of the situation and of your emotions, then you can control your behaviour to remain in control. Stress can lead to loss of self-control and your behaviour will revert to being dominated by your personality.

- **A little knowledge can be dangerous:** it requires time to understand personality and how it translates into behaviour, and this is best left to the experts. It is easy to make incorrect assumptions or to fall into the trap of stereotyping.

- **There is no time to apply this knowledge:** during preparation for the negotiation there is neither time nor opportunity to perform multiple personality tests on members of the other party's team. And, in the heat of the negotiation event, trying to apply what you do know about the personality of the other party and use it to your advantage is not at all easy. Instead, careful observation of actual behaviour is likely to be more fruitful.

- **Always check assumptions by observing behaviour:** you might start with assumptions of what you know about someone's personality, if you do not know them. However, as soon as the negotiation event gets under way you can observe actual behaviour; you should use this as your guide, and not your assumptions about personality.

- **Knowing about personality can be useful:** it can help you to realise the extent to which humans are different, and how these differences might affect their behaviour. You should apply what you learn to yourself as well as to your negotiating opposite numbers; the more you know about how your own behaviour is influenced by your personality, the better.

THE THOMAS-KILMANN CONFLICT MODE INSTRUMENT (TKI)

The TKI is a means of measuring conflict style, which is also appropriate in the context of a negotiation. It assesses an individual's behaviour in conflict situations: situations in which the concerns of two people appear to be incompatible.

This model of conflict-handling behaviour was adapted from "Conflict and Conflict Management" by Kenneth Thomas in *The Handbook of Industrial and Organizational Psychology*, edited by Marvin Dunnette (Rand McNally, 1976). Other valuable contributions in this field are the work by Robert Blake and Jane Mouton in *The Managerial Grid* (Gulf Publishing, 1964 and 1994) and the work of Jeffrey Rubin and Bert Brown in *The Social Psychology of Bargaining and Negotiation* (Academic Press, 1975). Further information about the tool itself is available from the TKI website: www.kilmanndiagnostics.com

The model works by describing a person's possible behaviour, when in a conflict situation, along two basic dimensions: assertiveness, the extent to which the individual attempts to satisfy his or her own concerns, and cooperativeness, the extent to which the individual attempts to satisfy the other person's concerns.

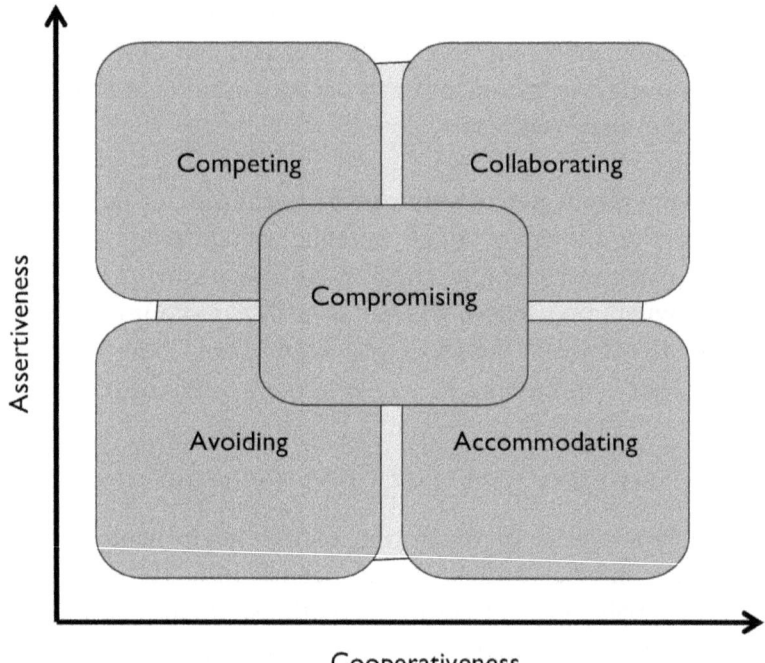

Cooperativeness

Diagram 8 – The Thomas Kilmann Conflict Mode Instrument

These two dimensions of behaviour can be used to define five separate methods of dealing with conflict, which are covered briefly below:

- **Competing:** this is assertive and uncooperative. When competing, an individual pursues their own concerns at the other person's expense, using whatever power seems appropriate to win by forcing their position onto the other person. Competing might mean standing up for your rights, defending a position you believe is correct, or simply trying to win.

- **Accommodating:** this is unassertive and cooperative, the opposite of competing. When accommodating, an individual neglects his or her concerns in order to satisfy the concerns of the other person; there is an element of self-sacrifice here. Accommodating might take the form of selfless generosity or charity, obeying another person's order when you would prefer not to, or yielding to another's point of view.

- **Collaborating:** this is both assertive and cooperative. When collaborating, an individual attempts to work with the other person to find a solution that fully satisfies the concerns of both. It involves digging into an issue to identify the underlying concerns of the two individuals and to find an alternative that meets both sets of concerns. Collaboration between two people might take the form of exploring a disagreement to learn from each other's insights, resolving some condition that would otherwise have them competing for resources, or confronting and trying to find a creative solution to an interpersonal problem.

- **Avoiding:** this is unassertive and uncooperative. When avoiding, an individual does not immediately pursue their own concerns or those of the other person; they simply do not address the conflict. Avoiding might take the form of diplomatically sidestepping an issue, postponing an issue until a better time, or simply withdrawing from a threatening situation.

- **Compromising:** this is intermediate in both assertiveness and cooperativeness. When compromising, an individual has the objective of finding an expedient, mutually acceptable solution that partially satisfies both parties. Compromising falls on the middle ground between competing and accommodating, giving up more than competing but less than accommodating. Likewise, it addresses an issue more directly than avoiding but doesn't explore it in as much depth as collaborating. Compromising might mean splitting the difference, exchanging concessions, or seeking a quick middle-ground position.

You will recognise some of these behaviours from the discussions on behaviour in chapter 4 of this book, particularly those of competing and accommodating, which we labelled as aggressive and passive. Trading behaviour is assertive, but otherwise does not fit this model. It is not truly compromising, as (instead of trying to find a middle ground that somehow satisfies each party) it tries to trade different things that have different values to each party, and therefore completely satisfy both parties. Compromising is often the behaviour used in negotiation to try to reach agreement when there is only one tradable. Collaborating and avoiding, are behaviours more suited to alternatives to negotiation as ways of solving a problem.

APPENDIX 9

Understanding culture

INTRODUCTION

There are many different ways of measuring cultural differences, for example:

- Cultural dimensions theory (five dimensions), explored in the work of Geert Hofstede.

- National culture differences (seven dimensions), explored in the work of Fons Trompenaars.

- Time, Space and Context, explored in the work of Edward T Hall.

These measure different aspects of culture, or sometimes the same aspects but in different ways.

It is important to note that humans are humans whatever their cultural backgrounds and if you look for similarities across cultures instead of looking for differences, there are just as many. Donald E Brown explored this in his book *Human Universals* (McGraw Hill, 1991).

Differences between individuals within cultures, or between subcultures within cultures, can be just as great as across cultures. In addition, differences in negotiating behaviour are sometimes incorrectly ascribed to cultural differences. For example, in totalitarian regimes where there is a shortage of goods, personal relationships (who you know rather than what you know) become an increasing factor in how such goods are distributed. What is simply due to a difference in the market could be mistaken as being due to the culture of the regime.

If you are interested in exploring a way of looking at culture and its effect on negotiating behaviour, then you should look at an appropriate model. A good model to use is the seven dimensions of culture set out in *Riding the Waves of Culture: Understanding Diversity in Global Business* (Nicholas Brealey, 2012) by Fons Trompenaars and Charles Hampden Turner. This model is briefly explained below. Another useful work in this field is *Global Negotiation: The New Rules* (Palgrave Macmillan, 2008) by John Graham and William Hernández Requejo. Jonathan O'Brien in his book *Negotiating for Purchasing Professionals* (Kogan Page, 2013) gives a useful summary of a variety of approaches to measuring cultural traits and provides a table where he lists these traits by country.

EFFECT OF CULTURE ON NEGOTIATION BEHAVIOUR

Understanding culture certainly has its role in negotiation, but it also has its limitations. Its biggest use would be if you could accurately predict aspects of someone's behaviour from knowing their culture. This is not easy, and a little knowledge here can be a dangerous thing. It is always better to observe behaviour and respond appropriately.

You should consider the following:

- **Negotiation works across cultures:** the negotiation process remains the same and the choices of behaviour remain the same. You may have to change your style but you won't have to relearn how to negotiate.

- **All people are different:** people's behaviour is affected by many things, including their culture. It can be equally affected by their personality, their mood and their personal circumstances.

- **Avoid cultural stereotyping:** cultural stereotypes abound, as do people who epitomise them. However, it is dangerous to assume that everyone from China is inscrutable or that all Italians are volatile.

- **Knowing about cultural differences is useful:** it helps things along, reduces the chances of misunderstanding and offence, and can speed up progress. You should apply what you learn to yourself, as well as to your negotiating opposite numbers; the more you know about how you are conditioned by your culture, the better.

- **A little knowledge is dangerous:** do not fool yourself into thinking that if you know a lot about somebody's cultural background, then you can predict their behaviour in a negotiation.

- **Always check assumptions by observing behaviour:** you might start with assumptions about how people's culture might influence their behaviour, but as soon as the negotiation event gets under way you can observe actual behaviour, and you should use this as your guide, and not your assumptions about the effects of culture.

- **Use local support:** when negotiating with people from a culture that is not yours, then it can be useful to have local support.

TROMPENAARS' SEVEN CULTURAL DIMENSIONS

Trompenaars' model of national culture differences is a framework for cross-cultural communication applied to general business and management. It uses seven dimensions to describe a culture, where each dimension can be thought of as a "culture-trait". It can be summarised as follows:

- **Universalism versus particularism:** universalism is about finding broad and general rules and, when no rules fit, it uses the best rule. Particularism, on the other hand, is about finding exceptions. When no rules fit, it judges the case on its own merits, rather than trying to force-fit an existing rule.

- **Analysing versus integrating:** analysing decomposes to find the detail. It assumes that the answer can be found in the details and that decomposition is the way to success. It sees people who look at the big picture as being out of touch with reality. Integrating, on the other hand, brings things together to build the big picture and assumes that if you have your head in the weeds you will miss the true understanding.

- **Individualism versus communitarianism:** individualism is about the rights of the individual. It seeks to let people grow or fail on their own, and sees group-focus as stripping the individual of their rights. Communitarianism, on the other hand, is about the rights of the group or society. It seeks to put the family, group, company and country before the individual and sees individualism as selfish and short-sighted.

- **Inner-directed versus outer-directed:** inner-directed is about thinking and personal judgement: the answer lies in our heads. It assumes that thinking is the most powerful tool and that considered ideas and intuitive approaches are the best way. Outer-directed, on the other hand, is about seeking data in the outer world. It assumes that we live in the "real world" and that is where we should look for our information and decisions.

- **Time as sequence versus time as synchronisation:** time as sequence sees events as separate items in time, sequenced one after another. It finds order in actions that happen one after the other. Time as synchronisation, on the other hand, sees events in parallel, synchronised together. It finds order in the coordination of multiple efforts.

- **Achieved status versus ascribed status:** achieved status is about gaining status through performance. It assumes individuals and organisations earn and lose their status through their everyday efforts, and that other approaches are recipes for failure. Ascribed status is about gaining status through other means, such as seniority. It assumes status is acquired by right rather than daily performance. It finds order and security in knowing where status is and remains.

- **Equality versus hierarchy:** equality is about all people having equal status. It assumes we all have equal rights, irrespective of birth or of whatever other gifts we have. Hierarchy is about people being superior to others. It assumes that order happens when few people are in charge and that others obey through a chain of command.

APPENDIX 10

Avoiding mistakes and dealing with hostile negotiators

INTRODUCTION

During the negotiation event, when the pressure is on, it can be difficult to behave as you ought. It pays, therefore to learn in advance about just what might happen. This appendix covers the following:

- **Mistakes:** a number of errors are made over and over again in negotiation.

- **Dealing with hostile negotiators:** sometimes, you will meet a hostile, often manipulative, negotiator.

MISTAKES

It is easy to make mistakes, but also easy to avoid doing so if you know the potential pitfalls and recognise them in advance. Here is a brief list, many of which have been covered in more detail in earlier parts of the book:

- **Irrational escalation:** responding to an aggressive move with an aggressive response that then elicits a further aggressive response etc. This usually frustrates both parties and deadlocks the negotiation. This spiral is irrational in that it leads to worse outcomes for both parties and should be broken early on.

- **Fixed pies:** regarding what is under discussion as fixed, particularly when only one issue is on the table, usually price. This means that value will have to be shared, usually to the disadvantage of one party. It is always best to search for other options and to create other tradables if possible.

- **Incorrect framing:** regarding things as a loss, rather than as a gain. Sellers tend to overvalue what they have to sell and see things as a loss, buyers tend to undervalue what they buy as they have yet to get any value from the item.

- **Underestimation:** underestimating your own power, authority, ability and strengths.

- **Overestimation:** overestimating the other party's power or knowledge of your weaknesses.

- **False assumptions:** assuming you know what the opposition wants or how they are thinking or feeling. You should always test assumptions as soon as you can.

- **Intimidation:** becoming intimidated by your opponent's prestige, rank, title or educational accomplishments.

- **Being overly influenced:** being overly influenced by traditions, precedents, statistics, forecasts, or cultural icons and taboos.

- **Overvaluation:** overvaluing what you have to offer. The value to the other party is what counts.

- **Misuse of power:** misusing power when you know you have it.

- **Unclear objectives:** not knowing clearly what you really want. If you don't know what you want then you will certainly get something else.

- **Long-term deals:** when circumstances can change, binding yourself too tightly to a deal can leave you wishing that you hadn't. You should always negotiate reasonable get-out clauses in long-term deals.

- **Asking questions you don't want the answer to:** "is that your final proposal?" invites the answer "yes" and stops the negotiation.

- **Not meaning what you say:** dishonesty and lying are very bad tactics; they destroy both trust and relationship. Bluffing should always be used with great care, and you should always have a plan of what to do if your bluff is called.

- **Making unilateral concessions:** this weakens your ability to trade that concession for something you value. It does not build goodwill and invites further taking.

- **Forgetting the whole:** the deal is about all the issues, linked together, and you should not allow single issues to be picked off and negotiated to your disadvantage. "Nothing is agreed until everything is agreed" is a good maxim.

- **Poor communication:** not realising the need to explain things clearly, listen carefully and summarise precisely.

- **Inadequate preparation:** not having all the facts at your fingertips.

DEALING WITH TOUGH/HOSTILE NEGOTIATORS

Sometimes you will meet a tough, aggressive or even hostile negotiator. These can be particularly difficult to deal with. Manipulative negotiators are often quite effective at convincing their opponents to agree to their demands. We tend to assume that we will be strong in the face of a tough negotiating partner, but research and experience shows that we are actually likely to back down in the heat of the moment. It can be extremely challenging to stand up to difficult people who may have an arsenal of weapons, including ridicule, bullying, insults, deception and exaggeration.

The principles of negotiation remain exactly the same, and here are a number of tactics you could employ to help:

- **Face the challenge:** do not give in, but try also to get beyond the fight back mentality as this will only lead to escalation. Be firm and do not be afraid of deadlock.

- **Separate behaviour from issue:** make it clear that their behaviour will have no influence on the issue. Make it clear also that you are willing to trade and that they will get nothing from you unless and until you get something from them.

- **Deal with issues on their merits:** make it clear too that you will deal with issues on their merits. For example, if faced with a demand for an outlandish price increase, gather facts about the market and about cost drivers and about what other suppliers are doing, and use these to try to deal with the issue objectively.

- **Explore their behaviour:** probe the other party's point of view. Explore whether there are any hidden reasons or constraints causing the behaviour, and try to get these out in the open so that they can be dealt with.

- **Listen as you normally would:** do not write off the other party as irrational or crazy or call them a bully. You have to deal with them, and this does not help. Instead, act as you normally would, and in particular listen to see whether you can get a clue about what is really going on.

- **Set standards of behaviour:** if necessary, share your feelings and try to discuss any behavioural issues, making it clear what you consider to be acceptable.

- **Name the ploy:** if necessary, make your feelings clear about what you think the other party is doing. Name the ploy and make it very clear that you know exactly what is going on.

- **Get a reality check:** bring other members of your organisation into the negotiation and use them to check that it's not just you. Encourage the other party to do the same, in the hope that the presence of newcomers will modify the behaviour.

- **Be aware that some people do negotiate in bad faith:** it happens, and some people find it clever and acceptable to agree to something they have no intention of carrying out.

- **Take only small risks:** when faced with someone you do not trust, do not be too trusting. Break large risks down into sums of small risks if you can, and proceed one step at a time.

- **Be creative:** in the face of excessive demands, try to create as many proposals as possible. Maybe the response to one of these will be helpful.

- **Offer a concession:** just occasionally it might be right to break the no-concession-without-something-in-return rule, but only if this enables an issue to be sidestepped so that you can get on with the rest of the negotiation.

- **Say no and walk away:** if all else fails, be ready to walk away from the negotiation if you genuinely believe that to continue is not in your interest. In this case you will need a BATNA.

About the Authors

Steve Mallaband is an experienced procurement professional. Following a long and successful career as an international procurement manager he founded his own consultancy dedicated to building excellence in procurement in the business world. As a consultant he has lectured, given training, written about procurement, and provided hands-on buying expertise to a number of international clients.

Ros Howard is a highly skilled communications coach who believes that the art of communication is fundamental to excellence in business practice. Following a successful industrial career, she has dedicated herself to working with native and non-native English speakers to improve their written and oral communication skills.